# INSECTS

HOW IT WORKS

# INSECTS

GERALD LEGG

Cavendish Square

Published in 2025 by Cavendish Square Publishing, LLC
2544 Clinton Street, Buffalo, NY 14224



Website: cavendishsq.com



Series Editor: Elizabeth Miles
Illustrations: Steve Weston
Additional illustrations: Ruth Lindsay, Jim Channell
Photography and additional illustrations: Shutterstock.com (Mikado767, Aksenova Natalya, Yusnizam Yusof, irin-k, Juraj Kovac, D. Kucharski K. Kucharska, Vladimirkarp, suns07butterfly, Malachi Jacobs, Sergey Toronto, Ultraviolet_Photographer, Cherdchai Chaivimol, alslutsky, bluehand, pzAxe, Africa Studio, Protasov AN, Kirsanov Valeriy Vladimirovich, Super Prin, IrinaK, Tyler Fox, Matt Jeppson, Shutter Rich, Cosmin Manci, goldenjack, epioxi, Pavel Krasensky, Eric Isselee, SSalparadis, Hector Ruiz Villar, thomas eder, DJTaylor, MeggedyannePhotography, PHOTO FUN, Pavel Mikoska, Scadidi, khunkorn, thatmacroguy, HHelene); Ajcoyote (CC BY-SA 3.0); Greg Hume (CC-BY-2.5)

Cataloging-in-Publication Data

Names: Legg, Gerald.
Title: Insects / Gerald Legg.
Description: Buffalo, NY : Cavendish Square Publishing, 2025. |
Series: How it works | Includes index.
Identifiers: ISBN 9781502671912 (pbk.) | ISBN 9781502671929 (library bound) |
ISBN 9781502671936 (ebook)
Subjects: LCSH: Insects--Juvenile literature.
Classification: LCC QL467.2 L44 2025 | DDC 595.7--dc23

CPSIA compliance information: Batch #CSCSQ25: For further information contact Cavendish Square Publishing LLC at 1-877-980-4450.

Printed in the United States of America

# Contents


What Is an Insect? 6
Armor Plating 8
Insect Eyes 10
Feelers 12
Flying 14
Hunting 16
Self-defense 18
Color and Shape 20
Feeding 22
Parasites 24
Mating 26
New Life 28
Changing Shape 30
Ant Nest 32
Bee Nest 34
Rainforest Life 36
Insects in Water 38
Woodland Life 40
Desert Insects 42
Microscopic Life 44
Index 46


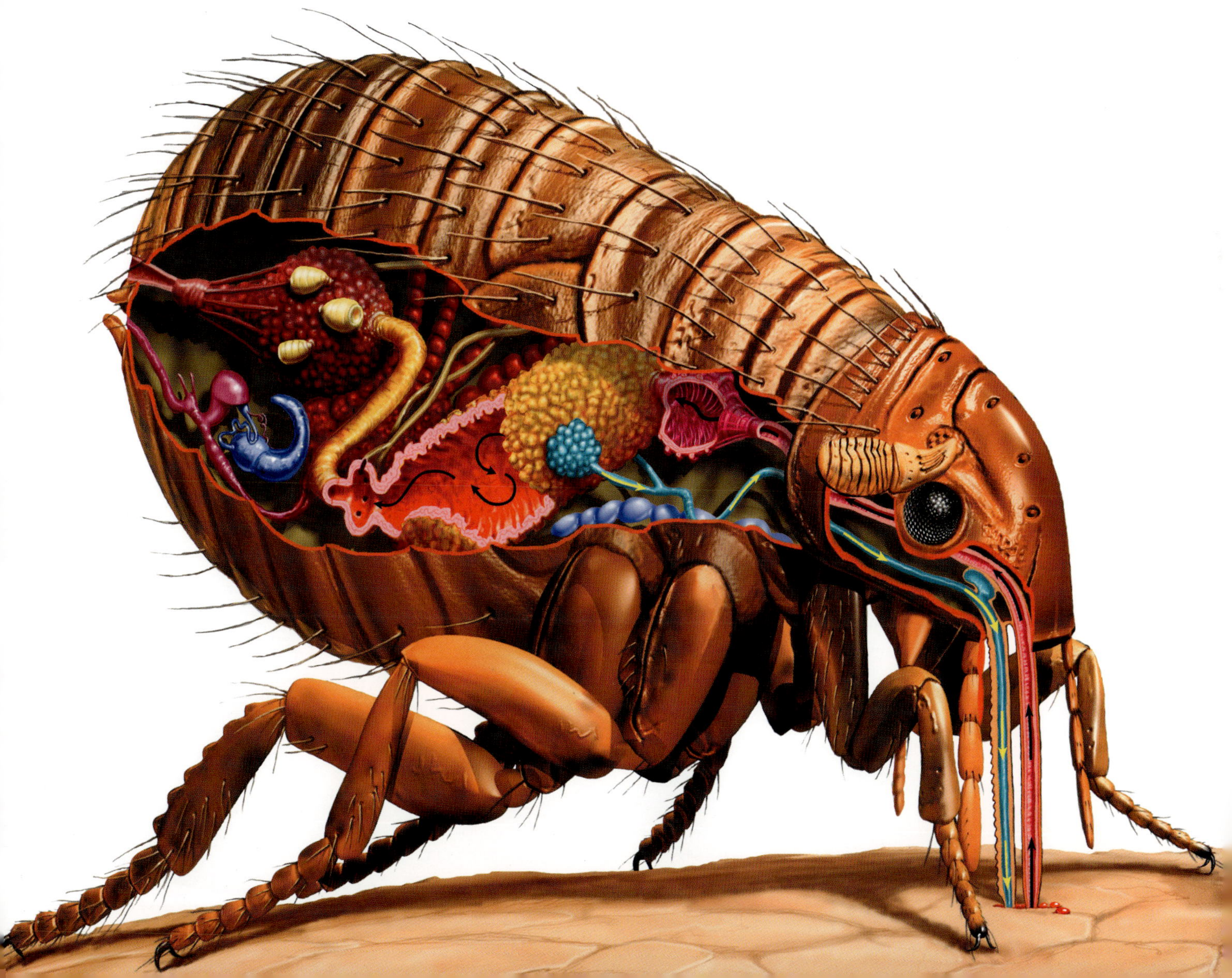

# What Is an Insect?

There are more insects on Earth than any other type of creature. Insects are strong and small, with three pairs of legs but no backbone. Like knights in armor, they have a tough outer covering. This outer skeleton (exoskeleton) supports and protects the insect's body parts and soft insides.

The protected head of an insect holds the brain and carries the antennae, eyes, mouth, and special jaws. Different insects have differently shaped jaws, allowing them to eat all kinds of things. The abdomen contains the main organs, including those for digesting food. Throughout the body, special breathing tubes called trachea carry air to and from the body's tissues. A long, thin heart circulates blood. A nerve cord that controls various body processes runs from the brain to the tip of the abdomen.

## How does a locust jump?

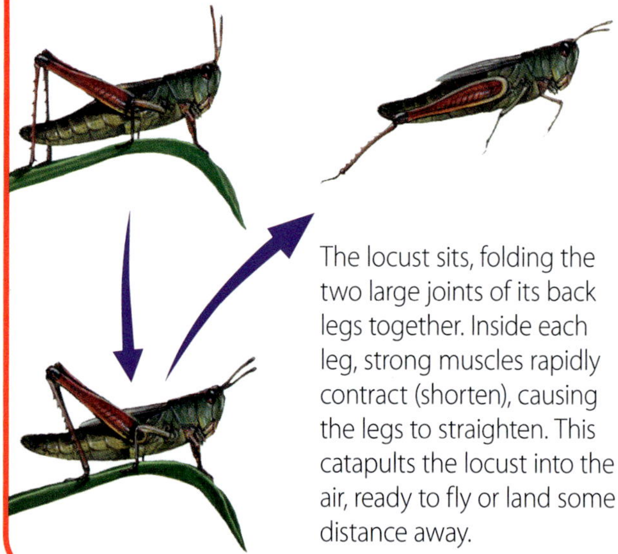

The locust sits, folding the two large joints of its back legs together. Inside each leg, strong muscles rapidly contract (shorten), causing the legs to straighten. This catapults the locust into the air, ready to fly or land some distance away.

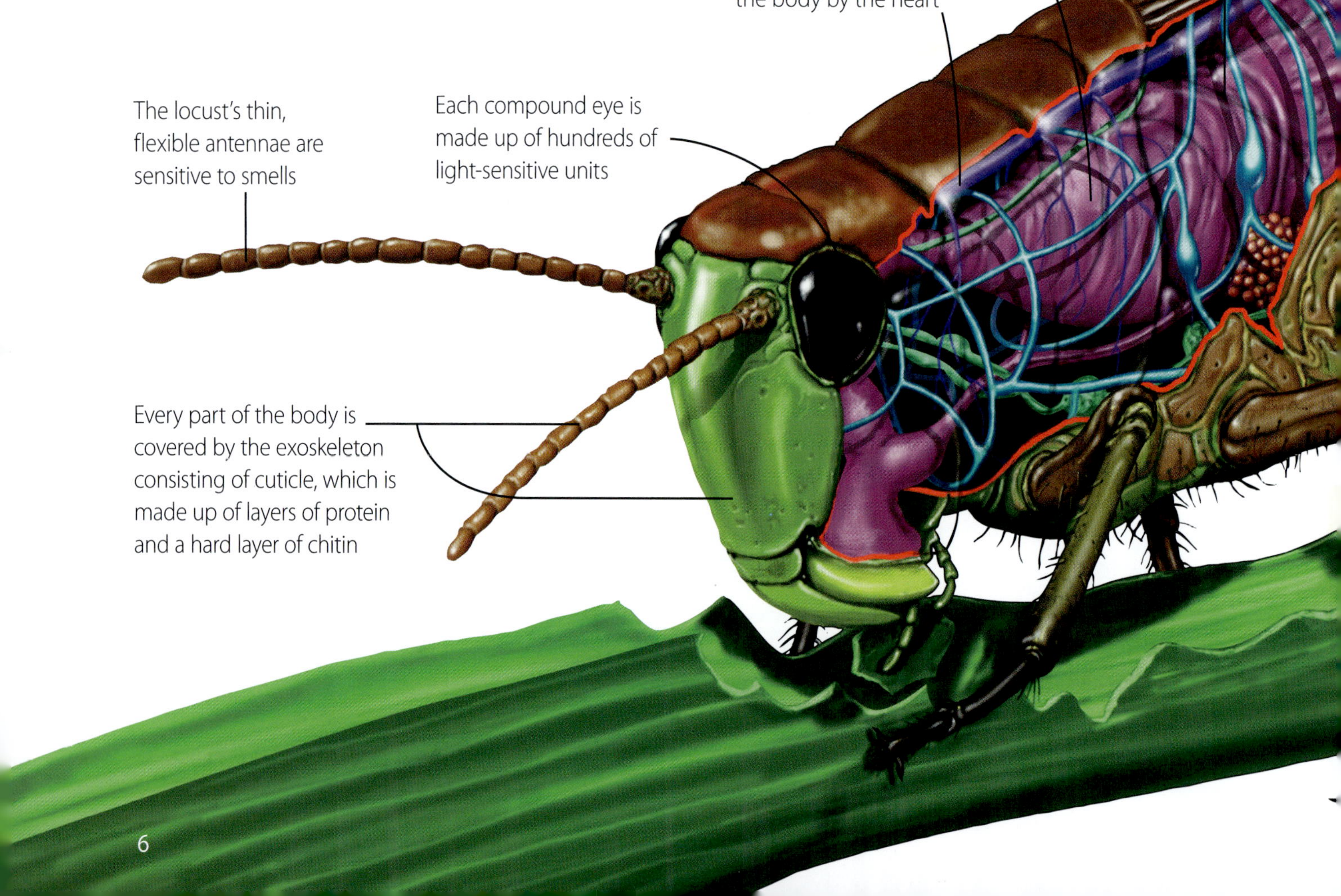

## Making sound

Locusts and grasshoppers chirp by rubbing a scraper (on the inside of the middle segment of each back leg) against special veins on the forewings.

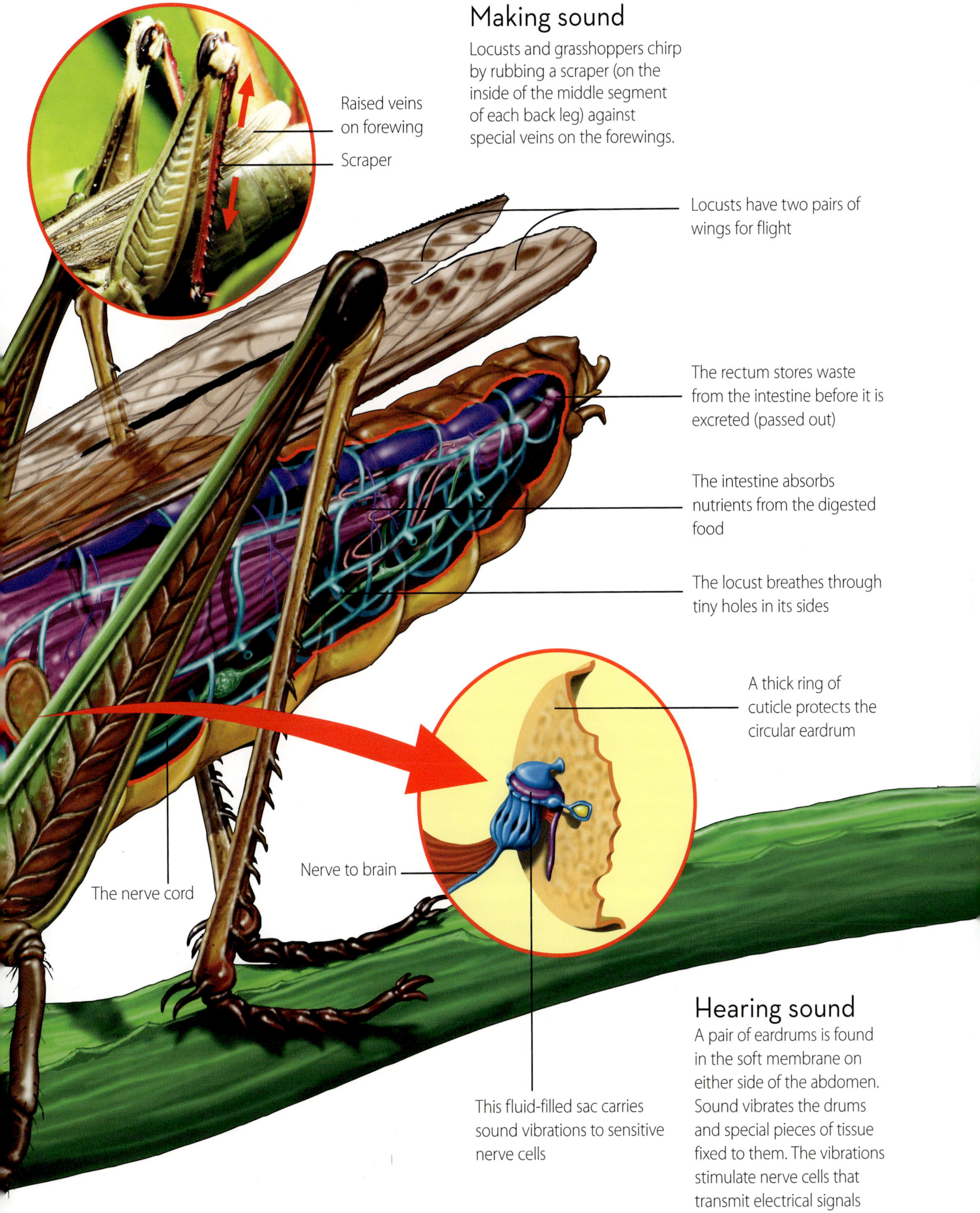


## Hearing sound

A pair of eardrums is found in the soft membrane on either side of the abdomen. Sound vibrates the drums and special pieces of tissue fixed to them. The vibrations stimulate nerve cells that transmit electrical signals to the brain.

# Armor Plating

Insects wear their skeleton on the outside, like armor. This exoskeleton is what makes insects so good at survival, even in conditions that are too extreme for other kinds of animals. Made of cuticle, it is tough and skinlike, protecting the organs and supporting the muscles. The cuticle itself constists of layers of protein and a layer of ultra-hard chitin.

Insects' jaws are covered in cuticle that is very hard, except at the joints, where it is soft and flexible. Thin tubes of cuticle make strong, jointed legs. The head and thorax are like boxes made of thick cuticle.

The head protects the brain and carries the sense organs and mouthparts. The strong thorax supports the wing and leg muscles. In contrast, the abdomen, which holds most of the body organs, is flexible and made of rings of cuticle, called segments.

## Beetles

There are over 350,000 species of beetles ranging in size from 0.02 inch (0.5 mm) to over 6.7 inches (170 mm). They are found everywhere. Hard, tough forewings protect their delicate flying wings. Shown here is a spotted flower beetle.

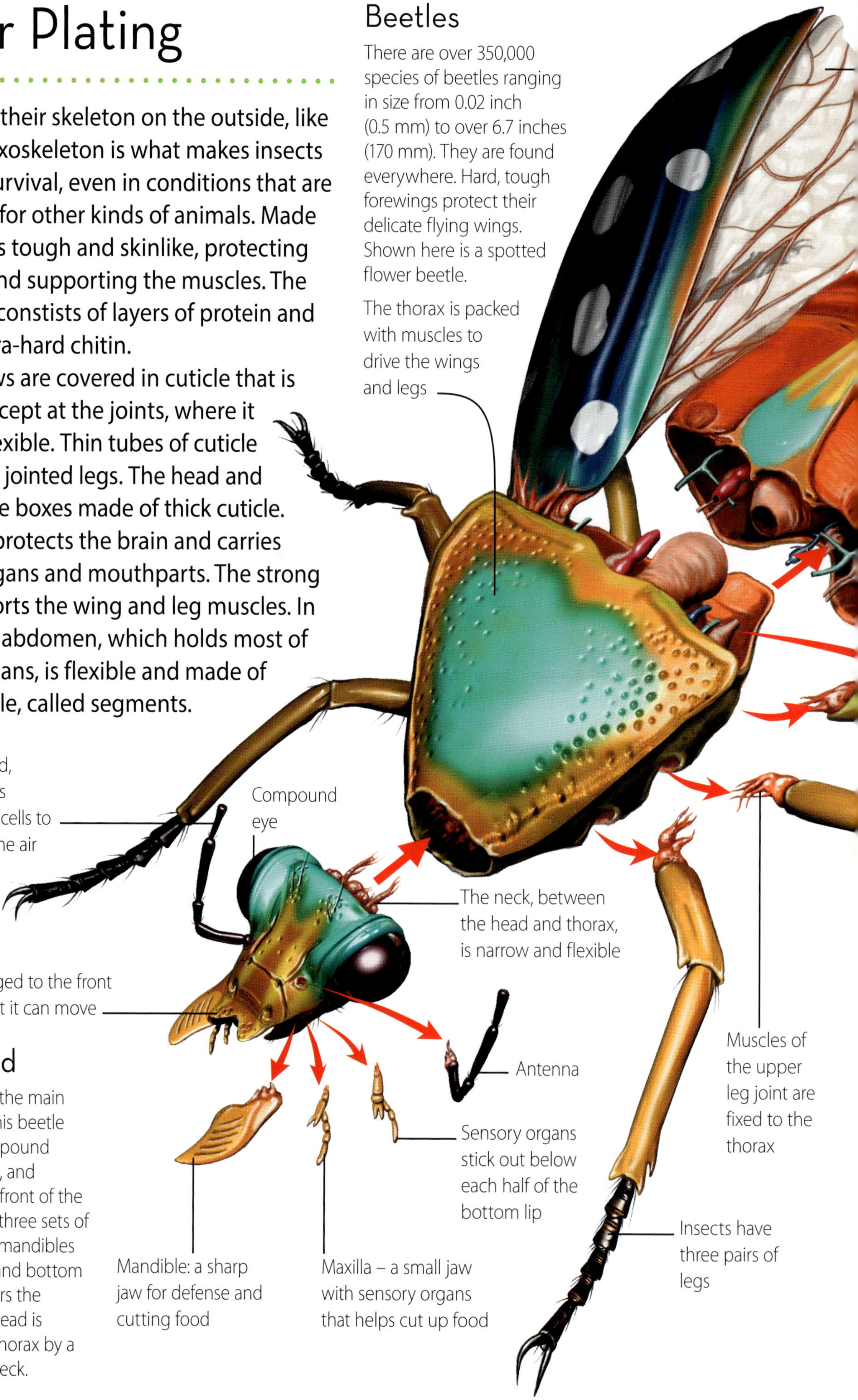


## Insect head

The head carries the main sense organs – this beetle has a pair of compound eyes, simple eyes, and antennae. At the front of the mouth there are three sets of mouthparts: the mandibles (jaws), maxillae, and bottom lip. A top lip covers the mandibles. The head is attached to the thorax by a narrow, flexible neck.

## Exoskeleton

The exoskeleton is made up of the cuticle and the epidermis. The cuticle consists of layers of strands of long, sugar-like molecules embedded in a hardened substance, like steel rods in concrete. Cells in the epidermis secrete the waxy top layer that waterproofs the insect. Sensory cells and bristles also form part of the exoskeleton.

## Joints and hinges

In order to move around easily, insects need joints in their armor-like skeleton. Each leg, wing, mouthpart, and antenna is jointed, and connects to the body with a hinge or ball-and-socket joint. Between the joints the cuticle is soft and flexible, allowing for movement. So that an insect can move along uneven surfaces, each leg joint is hinged at a slightly different angle to its neighbor. The wings have complicated hinges where they join the thorax. In beetles, even the wings themselves have hinges. These lie between the veins and allow the wings to be folded away underneath the protective forewings.

# Insect Eyes

Insects have two types of eyes. The largest are the compound eyes that appear as a honeycomb pattern of hexagons when seen under a microscope. Each hexagon is the transparent cuticle of an individual organ of sight. Insects can have as many as 30,000 of these in each compound eye or as few as one. Each of these sight organs (called ommatidia) sees only a tiny part of the surroundings. But as the tiny images are merged in the brain, the insect is able to see all around in great detail.

The second type of eyes, called ocelli, are usually much smaller. They are similar to human eyes, but cannot see an image. Instead, they are very sensitive to light. Nocturnal insects, which are active at night, have very large ocelli.

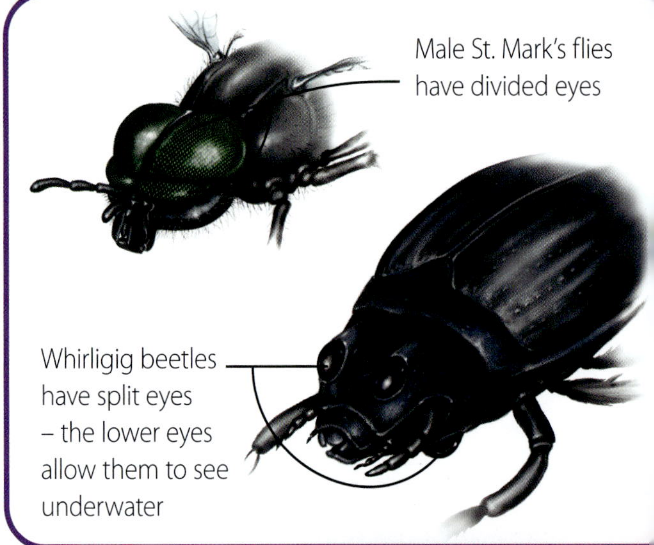

## Ommatidia

Light from the outside world enters each ommatidium and is focused by a hexagonal lens. It then passes through the crystal-like cone that also helps to focus it. Next, it reaches the nerve cells, which have a light-sensitive inner part. From here, the light is carried by nerve fibers to the brain. Pigment cells surround the nerve cells and stop light leaking into the rest of the eye, as this would spoil the image.

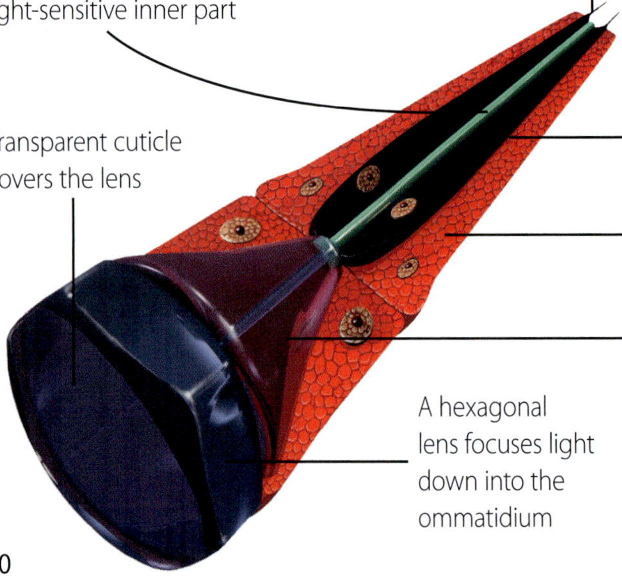

## Unusual eyes

Whirligig beetles live on the surface of ponds. Their eyes are split, with one pair on top and the other underneath. This lets them see above and below the water's surface at the same time. The eyes of male St. Mark's flies are divided into an upper part with large ommatidia and a lower part with small ommatidia.

## Damselfly

Damselflies are delicate but agile hunters. Large compound eyes (1) provide very clear, all-round vision. Light-sensitive ommatidia (2) send their mass of signals down the huge optic nerves (3) to the brain (4), which analyzes information from all the senses. The damselfly's three small ocelli (5) are sensitive to light intensity. They are situated between the widely spaced compound eyes.

## Invisible color

Many insects can see ultraviolet, a color invisible to us. Some flowers reflect this color so that insects can see special markings that will guide them to the flower's nectaries.

# Feelers

Insect feelers are remarkable instruments. The two feelers (antennae) are covered in many thousands of sensory cells, which can detect tiny amounts of chemicals, even a single molecule. This means, for example, that a male moth can detect the scent of a female moth that is over 0.6 mile (1 km) away.

Insects can even "see" using their feelers, mapping out the shape of their surroundings from the smells in it. Insects use sensory cells to find their way around and to find many other things: a mate; the right plant on which to lay their eggs; tasty prey, or a good host to live on. Although insects have other chemical-sensitive organs, such as taste organs, these are not as sensitive and need direct contact with a substance.

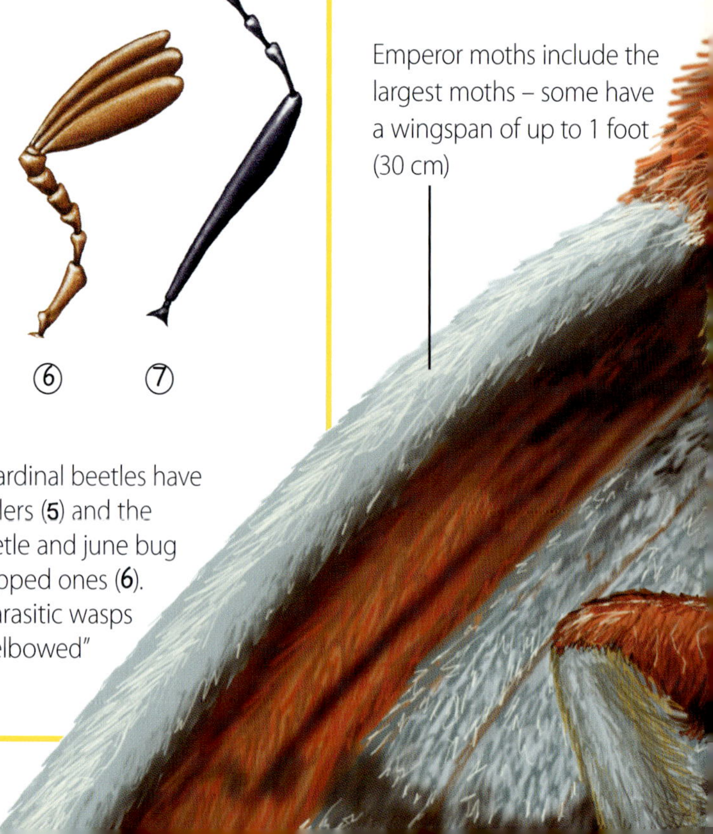


## Types of feelers

Feelers come in a great variety of shapes and sizes, especially in the beetle world. Springtails and dragonflies have thread-like feelers (**1**). Some ground beetles have a saw-edge variety (**2**). Termites and earwigs have bead-like ones (**3**) and those of burying beetles are clubbed (**4**). Sawflies and cardinal beetles have feather-like feelers (**5**) and the cockchafer beetle and june bug have feather-tipped ones (**6**). Weevils and parasitic wasps have flexible "elbowed" feelers (**7**).

## Sensory peg

Thousands of sensory pegs on each antenna detect scent molecules in the air. The molecules enter through pores and touch the sensitive parts of a sensory cell, which recognizes them. The information is sent to the antenna's main nerve and then to the brain.

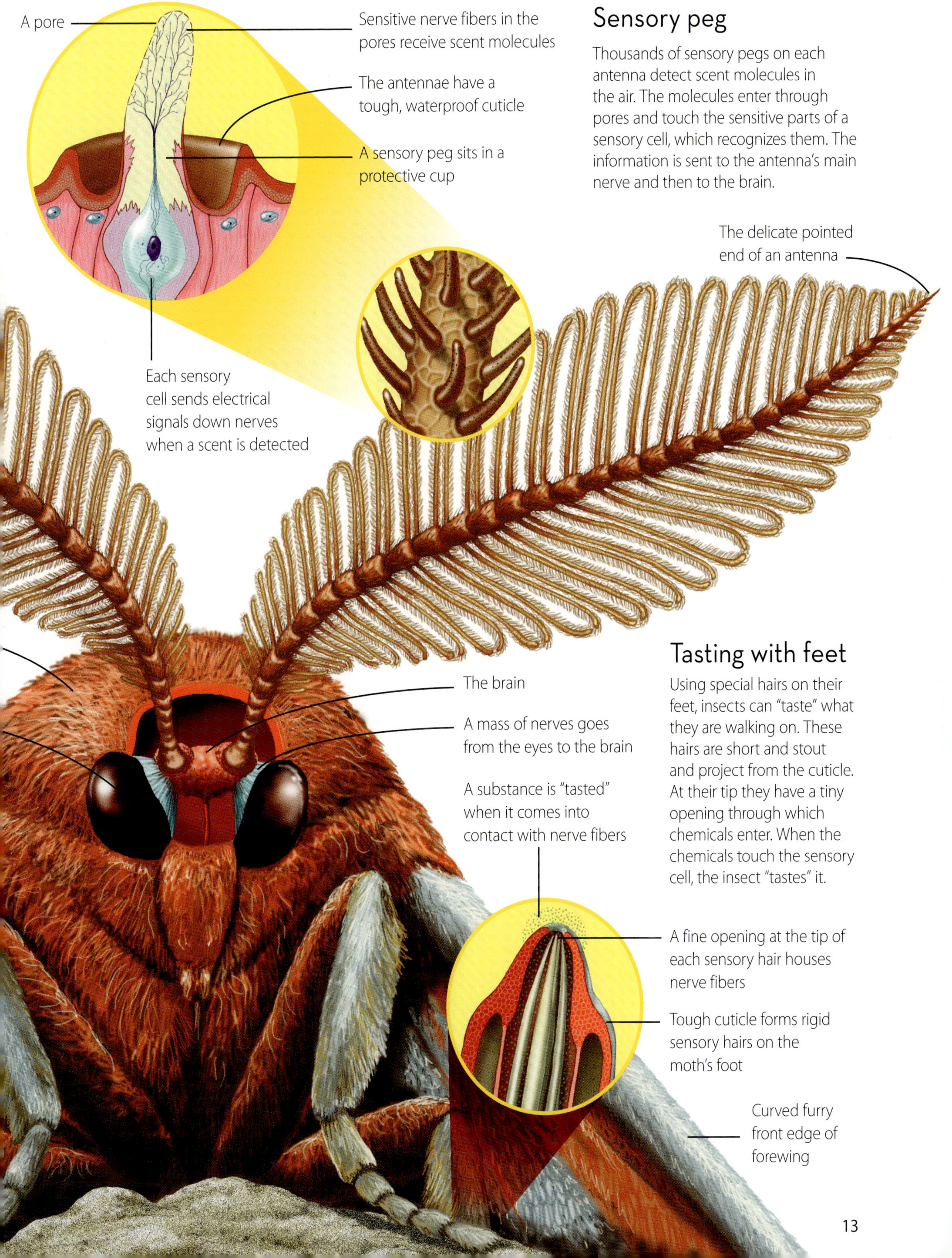


## Tasting with feet

Using special hairs on their feet, insects can "taste" what they are walking on. These hairs are short and stout and project from the cuticle. At their tip they have a tiny opening through which chemicals enter. When the chemicals touch the sensory cell, the insect "tastes" it.

# Flying

Insects can perform almost any flying maneuver – forwards, backwards, sideways, or upside down. They can loop, hover, swoop, and even do vertical takeoffs. An insect's thorax is an extremely complicated, tough – but flexible – powerhouse, packed with muscles that control the movement of the wings. Each wing is hinged to the thorax by ball-and-socket joints that pivot near the inner end of the wing.

When the wing moves, it rocks on these joints like a seesaw that can swivel in all directions. To move their wings, some insects, including dragonflies, use muscles fixed directly to the end of their wings. Most other insects use muscles that are fixed to the top and bottom and the front and back of the thorax.

## Wing types

The dragonfly (1) has two pairs of wings that move alternately. They are driven by muscles fixed directly to the wings. A butterfly (2) has slow-beating wings that overlap – the front wing pulls the back one down. Flies (3) use one pair of wings for flying, and a second pair form special organs for controlling flight. Beetles (4) have tough front wings that protect the delicate hindwings when they are folded away.

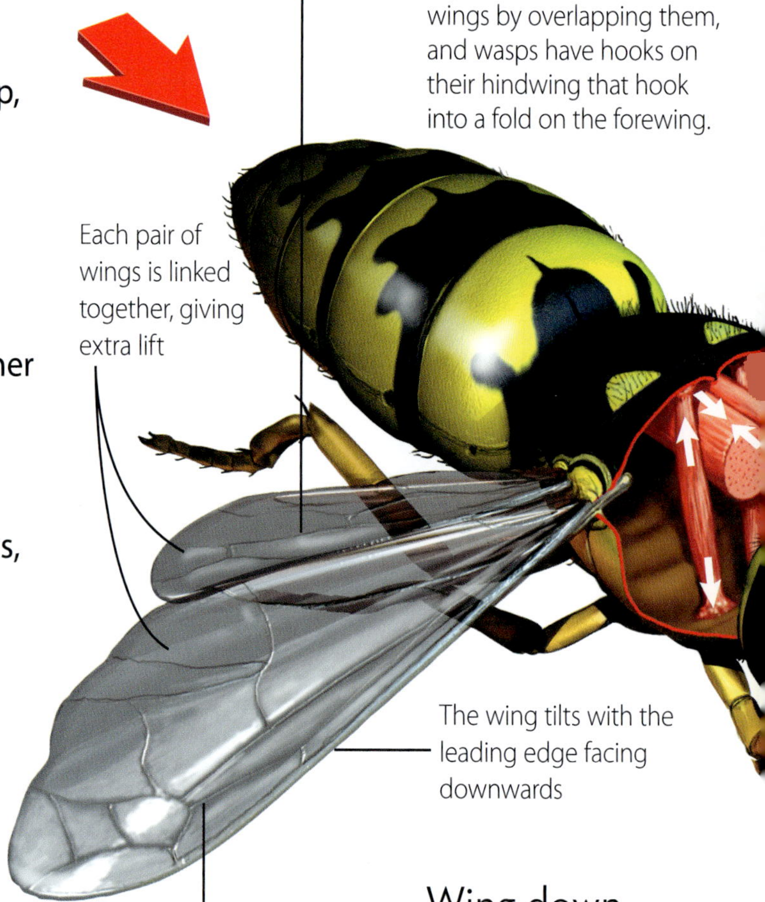

As the wasp moves forwards and lifts into the air, its wings beat up and down

Each pair of wings is linked together, giving extra lift

The wing tilts with the leading edge facing downwards

Veins give the wing strength and shape for efficient flight

On the upstroke, the wing tilts upwards

## Linked pairs

Wings that are linked together make for efficient flight. Butterflies link their wings by overlapping them, and wasps have hooks on their hindwing that hook into a fold on the forewing.

## Wing down

Many insects, like this wasp, move their wings down by contracting (shortening) the thorax muscles that run front to back and relaxing (lengthening) those that run top to bottom. This makes the thorax bulge. The thorax cuticle (outer covering) is like tough elastic, so when it bulges, the wings are flicked down.

(1)

(2)

(3)

(4)

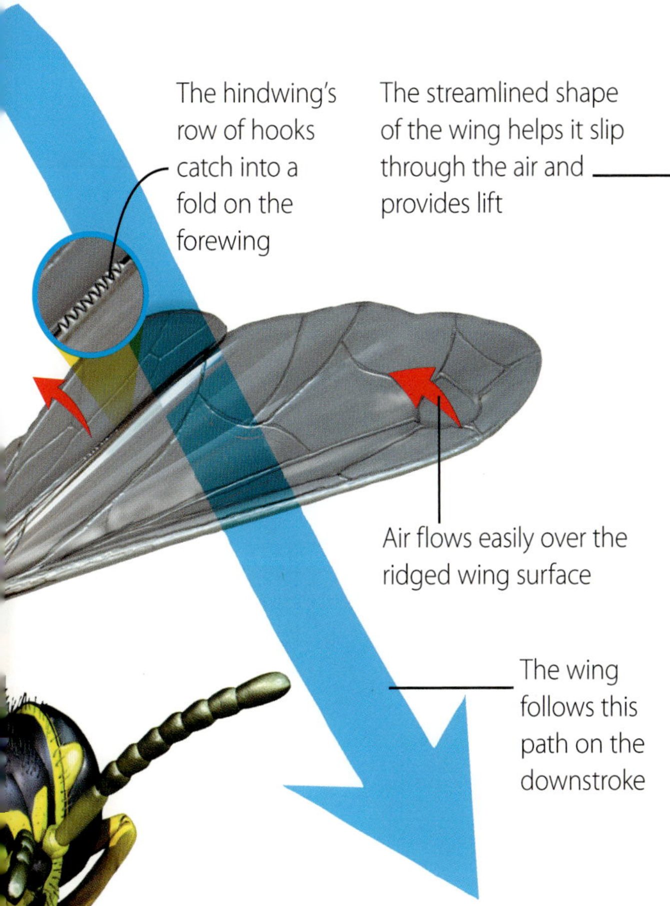


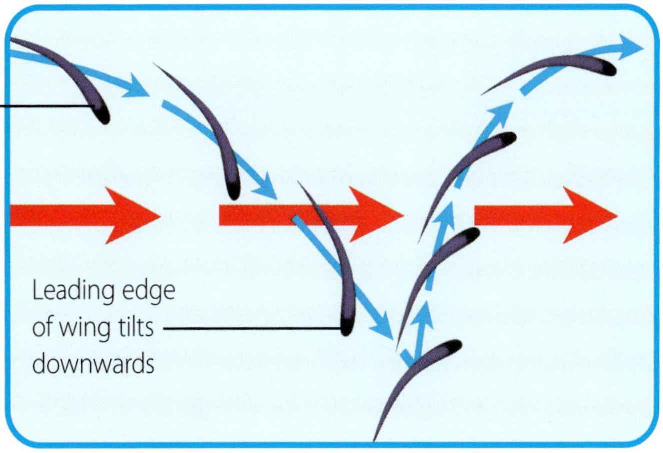


## Wing paths

Insects get their lift (power to keep them up in the air) from their up-and-down wing strokes. As the wing goes down, it tilts more and more. At the bottom of the stroke, it flicks around, its front edge facing forward. On the upstroke, this leading edge tilts forward again. By slightly tilting the wing in other directions the insect can change direction and maneuver precisely.

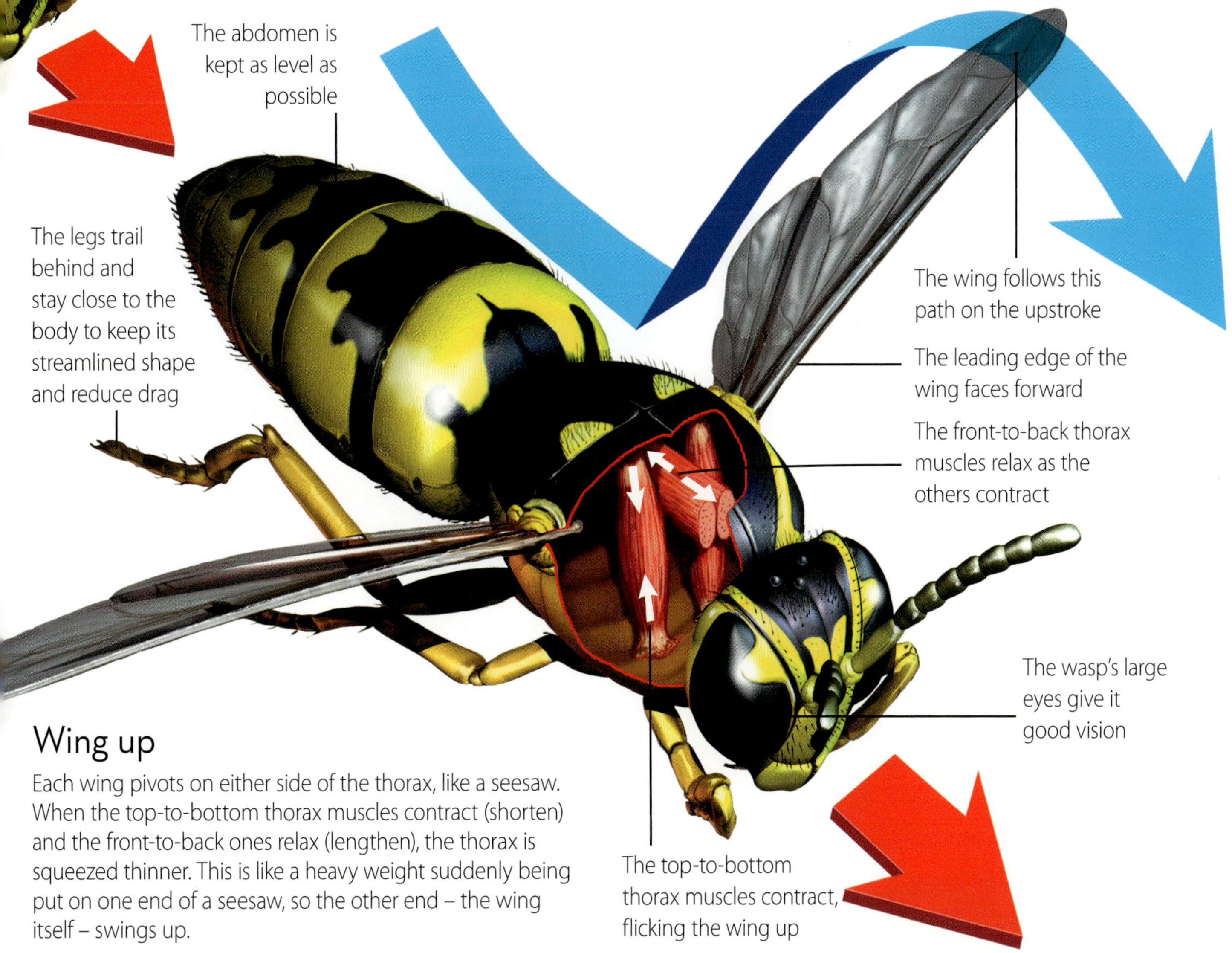


## Wing up

Each wing pivots on either side of the thorax, like a seesaw. When the top-to-bottom thorax muscles contract (shorten) and the front-to-back ones relax (lengthen), the thorax is squeezed thinner. This is like a heavy weight suddenly being put on one end of a seesaw, so the other end – the wing itself – swings up.

# Hunting

Predators need quick reactions and speed to catch wary or fast-moving prey. They are armed with powerful jaws, designed to capture, kill, and cut up their meal. Praying mantises (*right*) use their special front legs to catch their victims before biting their prey into pieces with their jaws.

Many insects are active hunters, prowling around looking for suitable prey. Others, such as mantises, employ a wait-and-see method. They patiently keep still until their victim comes within range, and then pounce on it. Such ambush hunters are well camouflaged to avoid being spotted by their victims until it is too late.

## Wait and see

A praying mantis keeps perfectly still, close to somewhere that its prey is likely to land. Its legs are bent, ready to pounce.

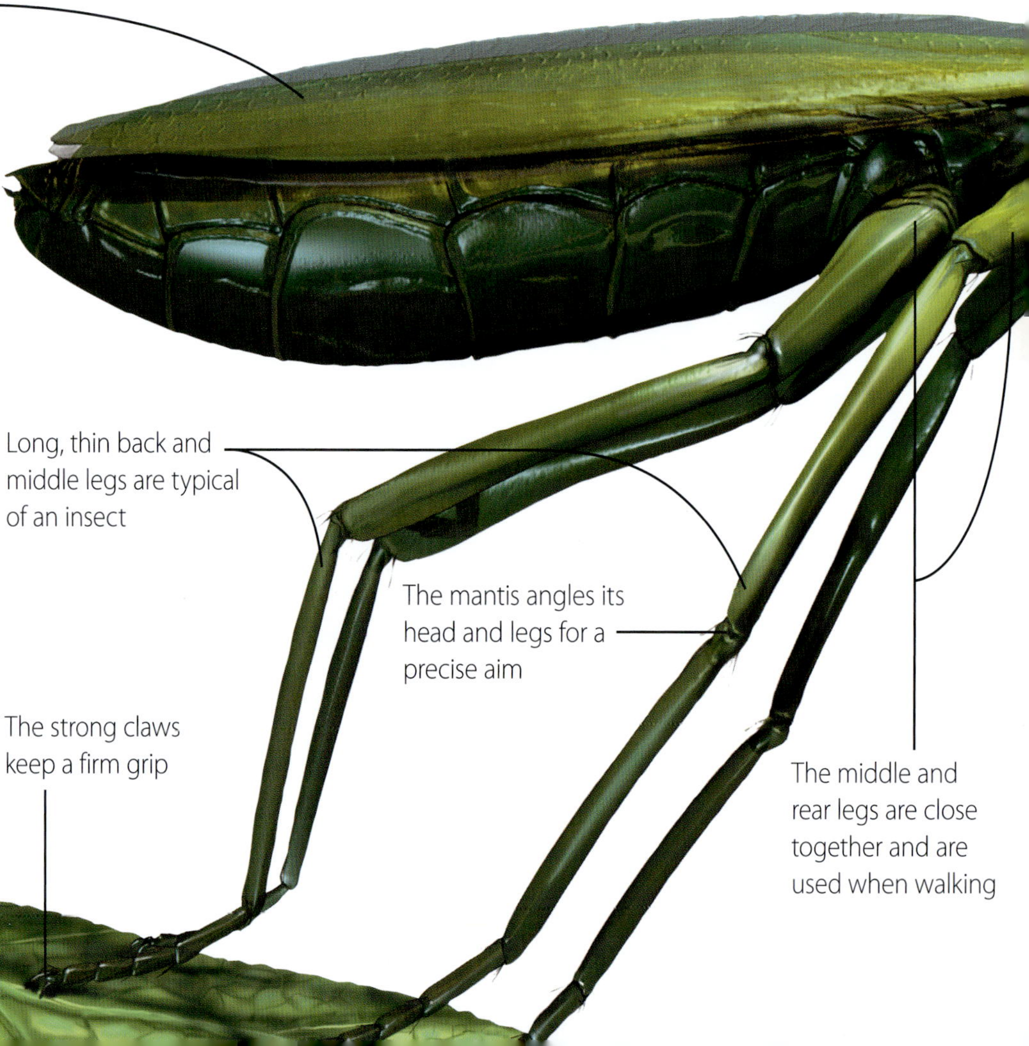


## In for the kill

The patience of the praying mantis is rewarded. With its keen vision, the praying mantis spots a bee landing on a flower. Using its claws, the mantis firmly grips its perch. Then, in the blink of an eye, its powerful back legs catapult its body forwards. At the same time, it shoots out its front legs and grabs the helpless victim, which has no time to avoid the unexpected, deadly lunge.

## Powerful jaws

Insect jaws have many uses. Soldier ants use them to catch food and to defend their colony. Tiger beetles use their jaws to catch their prey. The stag beetle's huge jaws are used in fighting and to attract a mate.

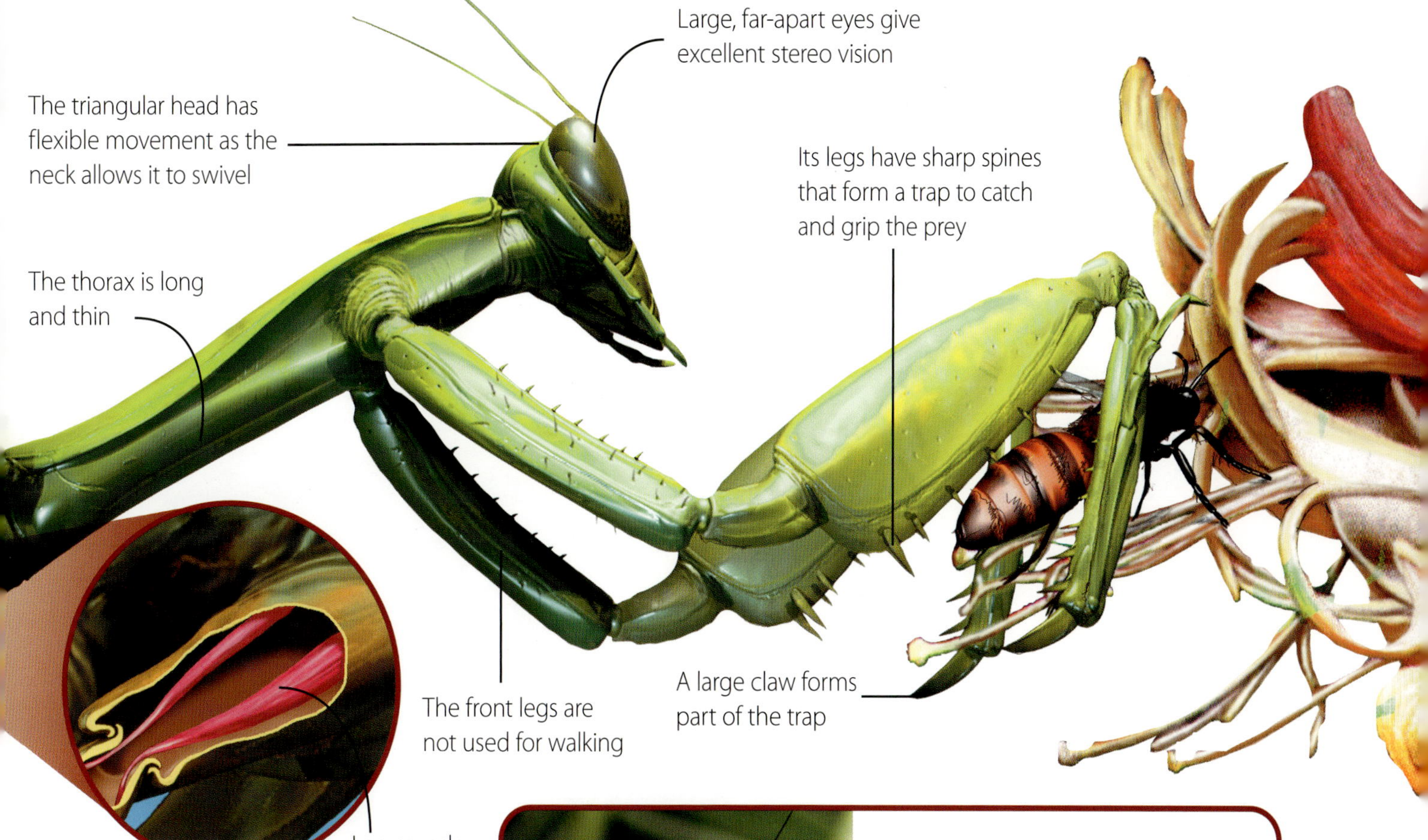



## Leg muscles

Strong leg muscles enable the mantis to keep perfectly still until it needs to move to catch its meal. Then the leg muscles rapidly straighten. The long body of the mantis allows it to reach prey that is some distance away without having to walk or run up to it, which could give the prey time to escape.

## Face-to-face

Large eyes high on a triangular head give the mantis excellent stereo (two-eyed) vision, so it can accurately judge distances. Its neck enables it to swivel its head to almost any angle. The mantis has sense organs on its neck and legs that enable it to determine exactly where to strike. Gripped in the spiny legs of the mantis, the victim is quickly passed to its mouth and sliced up by the mandibles.

# Self-defense

Many animals see insects as a tasty meal, so insects have to defend themselves. Some try to avoid their enemies by using camouflage, hiding, or running or flying away, but some face their predators. They may have armor that protects them – thick cuticle, a coat of spines, or poisonous hairs. Or they may be more active in their self-defense, with strong jaws to bite and stab, a painful (even deadly) sting, or the ability to produce a strong smell or loud noise that will drive a predator away. Some even secrete poisonous fluids, or, like the bombardier beetle (*right*), spray hot, irritating chemicals. Most of these masters of chemical warfare are brightly colored so predators know to leave them alone.

## Bombardier beetle

The bombardier beetle is built for speed. When it is not hunting, it lives under stones at the edges of fields. If disturbed or threatened in any way, it is well able to defend itself.

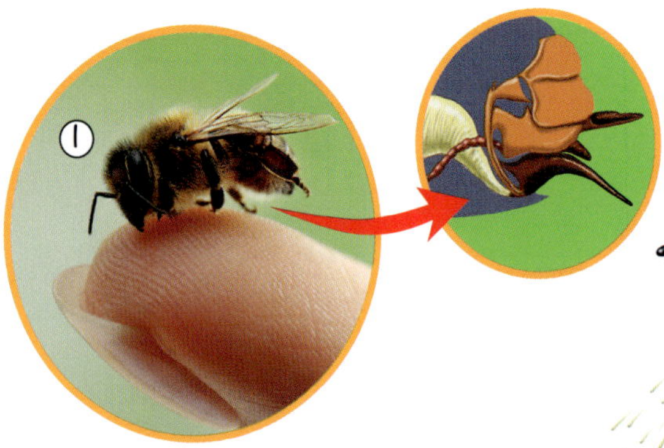


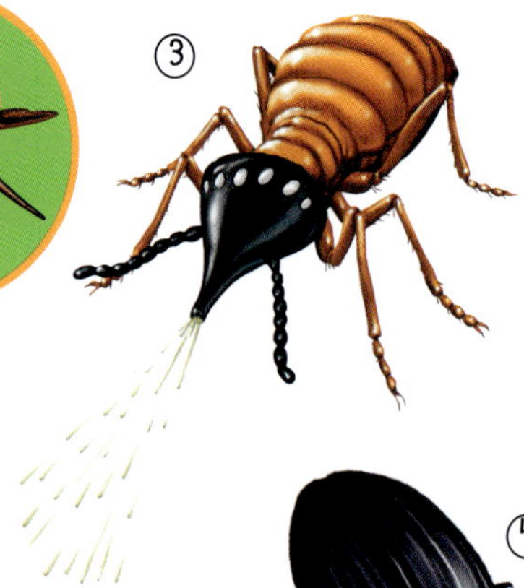

## Methods of defense

Female bees (1) are armed with a stinger. Glands in the bees produce a cocktail of irritating chemicals that can be pumped into a victim through a sharp, needlelike lance. Many moth caterpillars (2) are covered in spines or fine hairs, which serve as protection. The hairs are sharp and break off easily, causing intense irritation in the mouth of any predator. Some termite soldiers (3) squirt glue at predators to defend their colony. Instead of biting, they spray a sticky substance from their glands, which entangles the predator's legs and antennae. This leaf beetle (4) gives off an unpleasant drop of blood from its mouth when it is alarmed, which frightens birds, its main predator. When pursued by a bat (5), some moths emit squeaks and clicks. A bat uses sound (echolocation) to find its prey in the dark, and the moth's noises confuse its hearing, which gives the moth a chance to escape.

## Chemical warfare

Chemicals secreted by glands are stored in chambers. These storage chambers are separated from the explosion chambers by valves. When needed, the valves open and the chemicals are forced into the explosion chambers, detonated, and fired.

## Explosive chemicals

The glands produce several chemicals. The main ones are like chemicals used in some rocket engines. When mixed with enzymes, they react together, producing a hot, caustic (burning) spray.

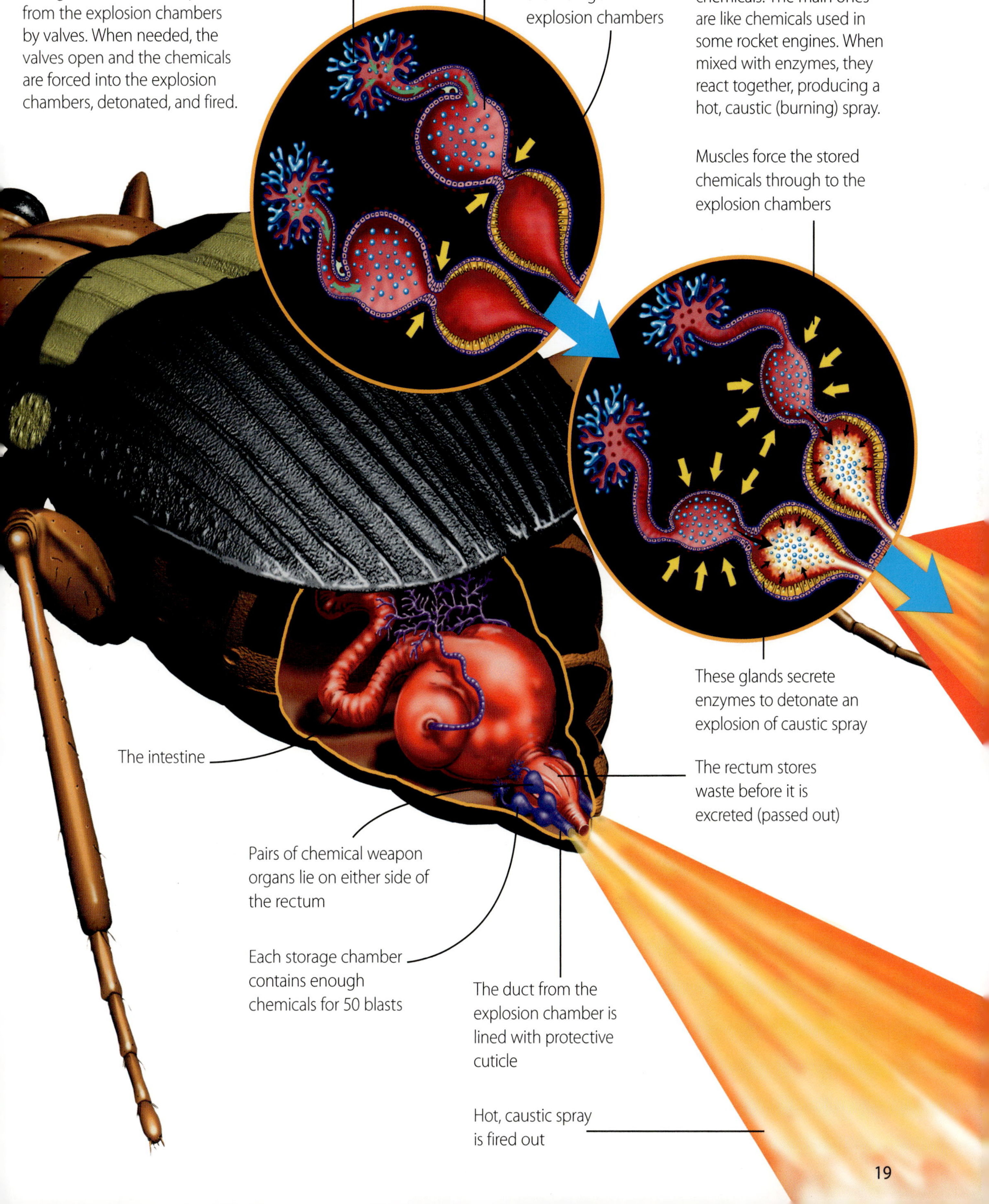

# Color and Shape

Insects are designed for survival. They come in a vast variety of colors and shapes, which help them avoid being eaten by predators. The folded wings of many butterflies are beautifully camouflaged, blending in with surrounding leaves, lichens, or tree bark. When open, the wings may use color in a different way. Vivid eyespot markings can startle a predatory bird. Bright yellows and reds on black can signal to predators that the butterfly tastes nasty, warning them to leave it alone. So, an insect's cuticle (outer covering) can be used for disguise or, like a flag, as a signal to other animals.

The colors and patterns can be produced with pigments (coloring in the wing tissue) and by the cuticle itself. White, blues, and greens are made by the shape of the surface of the cuticle. The varying combinations of pigment and cuticle give insects their distinctive and sometimes colorful armor.

## Morpho butterfly

Morpho butterflies flash blue as they fly through the sun-dappled South American rainforests, alternately exposing their colorful upper and camouflaged lower wing surfaces. The flashing attracts other morphos and confuses predators. When they are still, with their wings folded, eyespots on the wings' undersides can deter predators.

Eyespots startle predators

The wings' undersides are camouflaged to resemble dead leaves

White light shines onto the surface of the scales

Different-colored light is reflected from the ridges according to their depth

## Gleaming like gold

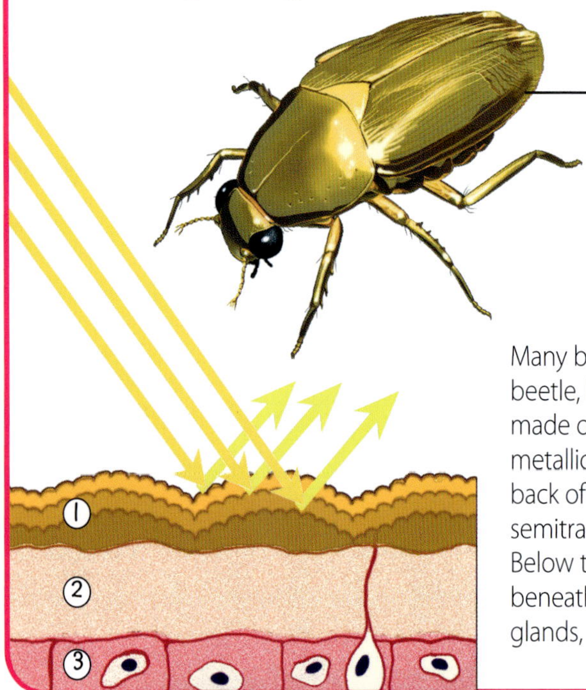


This beetle has gold camouflage because it lives on yellow flowers

Many beetles, such as this gold beetle, look as though they are made of metal. They owe their metallic coloring to light reflecting back off the different layers of their semitransparent outer cuticle (**1**). Below this is a softer cuticle (**2**), beneath which is a layer of cells, glands, and nerves (**3**).

## Colorful scales

A butterfly's wings are covered in thin, dust-like scales arranged in overlapping rows, like tiles on a roof. The scales are designed to color the surface of the wing and produce intricate patterns.

## Butterfly scales

Each butterfly scale is made up of parallel ridges, held up by supports. The ridges reflect each color – blue, green, and purple – in a different direction.

## Stick insects

Stick insects are aptly named. Their body, legs, and antennae are long and thin, resembling small sticks, making them very difficult to see. When they move, they are very slow.

## Insect twig

Many moth caterpillars, including "inchworms," are very thin and colored like plants. Holding on to a twig with their rear sucker-like legs, they often extend their body out stiffly, to imitate a shoot.

## Not what it seems

Some caterpillars and pupae have a strange way of disguising themselves. They pretend to be bird droppings – enough to put off any predator!

# Feeding

Insects can eat almost anything! They have versatile mouthparts that can cut, lick, and suck. Food is taken in through the mouth and enters the long alimentary canal, or gut, which is divided into three parts: the foregut, midgut, and hindgut.

Both the foregut and the hindgut are lined with a thin layer of cuticle. The foregut begins with the esophagus. This leads to the thorax, where it widens to form the crop. Food is stored in the crop before being passed on to the gizzard where it is ground up. The gizzard is lined with thick cuticle and spines or ridges. The midgut is not lined with cuticle, and digested food can be absorbed here. The hindgut is a coiled tube divided into three parts: the ileum, colon, and rectum.

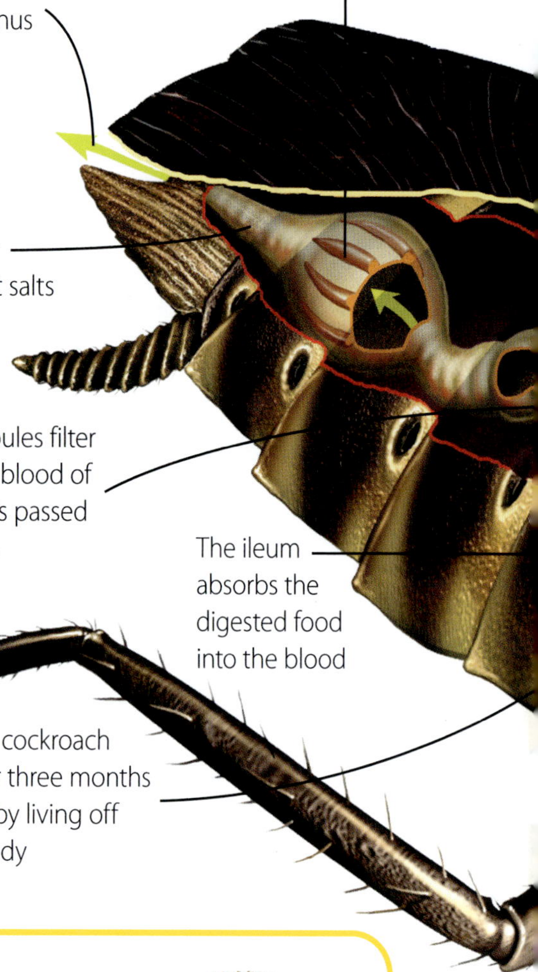


## Mouthparts

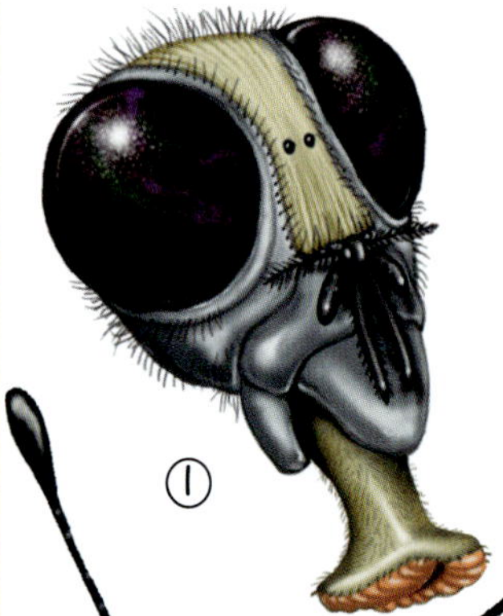
① 

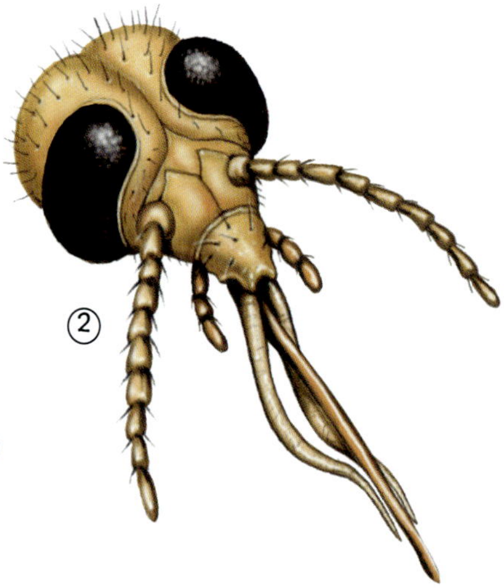
② 

④ 

③ 

A housefly (1) moistens its food with saliva first, then the food and saliva are sucked up. A mosquito's mouth (2) consists of a tube which contains a set of cutting tools. Females pierce the skin of their prey so blood can be sucked up. Males feed on plant juices. Butterflies (3) have an elongated, coiled mouthpart called a proboscis, which sucks up nectar. Bees (4) have licking and biting mouthparts. The mandibles can bite while the tongue can lap up nectar. Bush crickets (5) are scavengers and hunters. They have powerful mouthparts for biting and cutting.

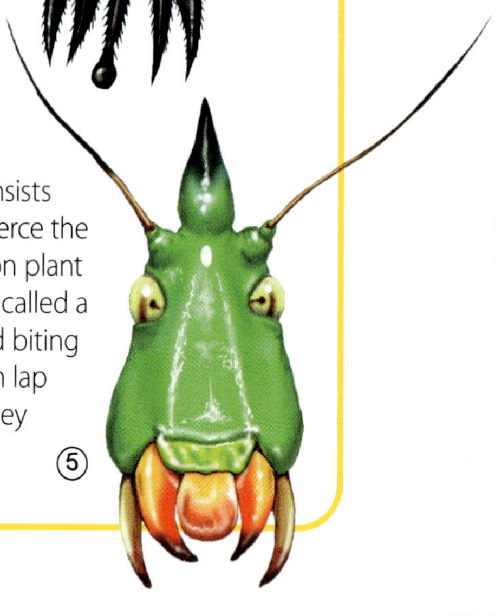
⑤

## Digestion

Cockroaches are omnivorous, eating scraps of food and other organic material. The salivary glands open near the mouth and pour saliva onto the food. As the food is chewed and mixed with saliva, the digestion of starch begins. In the crop, more enzymes (digestive juices) from the midgut are added. These digest proteins, fats, and sugars. In the gizzard, the food is ground up and digested further. Fine food particles enter the midgut, circulate, and are finally digested and absorbed. In the hindgut, water and important salts are absorbed before the indigestible waste leaves the body through the anus.

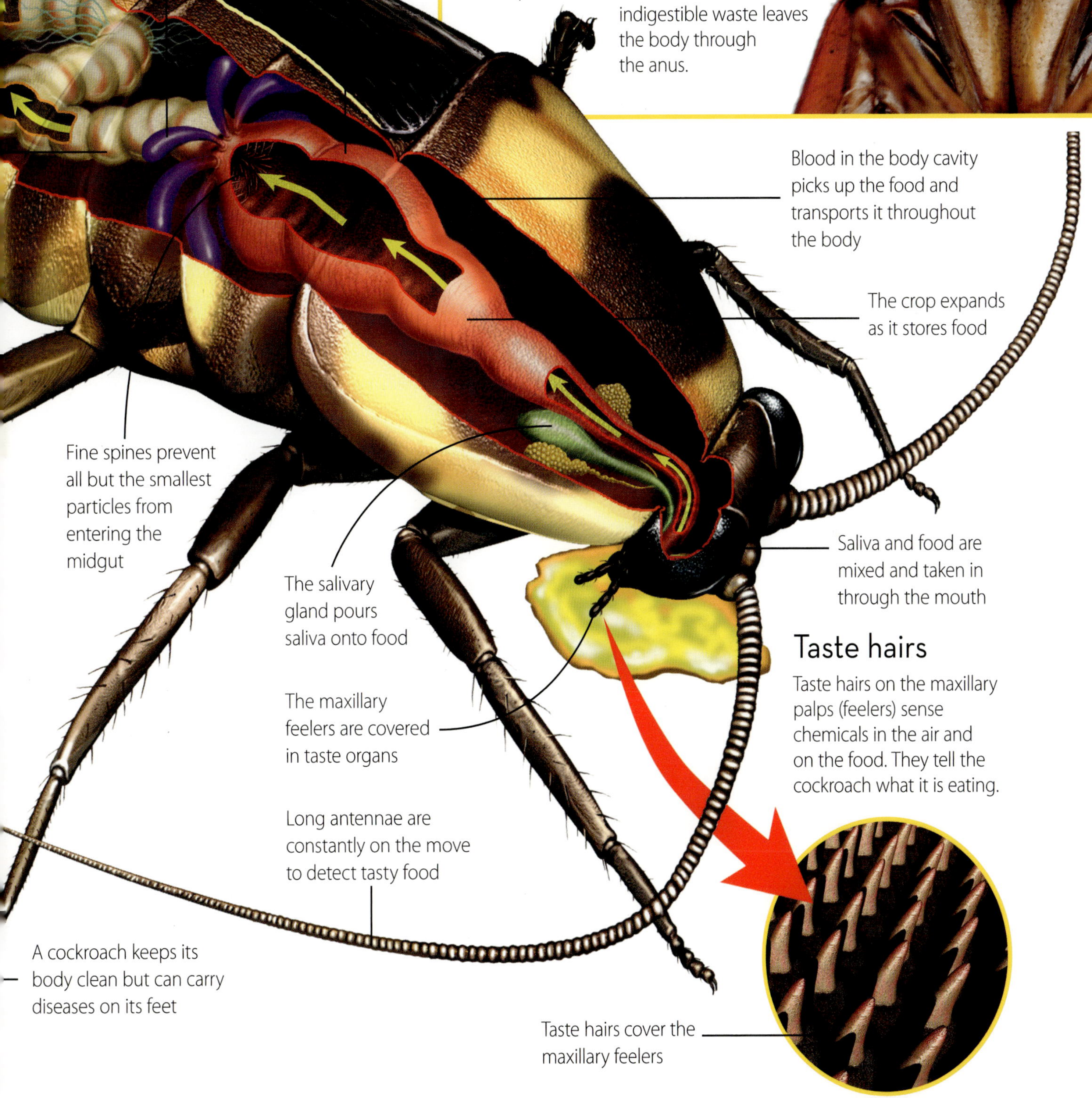


## Taste hairs

Taste hairs on the maxillary palps (feelers) sense chemicals in the air and on the food. They tell the cockroach what it is eating.

# Parasites

Blood from a living animal can make a tasty meal for some insects. Bloodsucking insects that live on other animals are called parasites. Their host is their food source, but living on another animal can be difficult. The host does not want them and will try to remove them. For example, to survive any attempt to be pulled or shaken off, a flea (*right*) has bristles, hairs, and hooks to help it grip the host's hair. Strong claws also grip the host's skin.

A flea's exoskeleton is very thick, tough, and slippery, making it hard for the host to squash or grip it. Using its powerful legs, it can jump away from danger and jump back onto its host. The flea's thin body enables it to squeeze between the host's hairs. Its mouthparts are able to penetrate the host's skin to reach the blood beneath and draw it up into the flea's expandable gut.

## Jumping legs

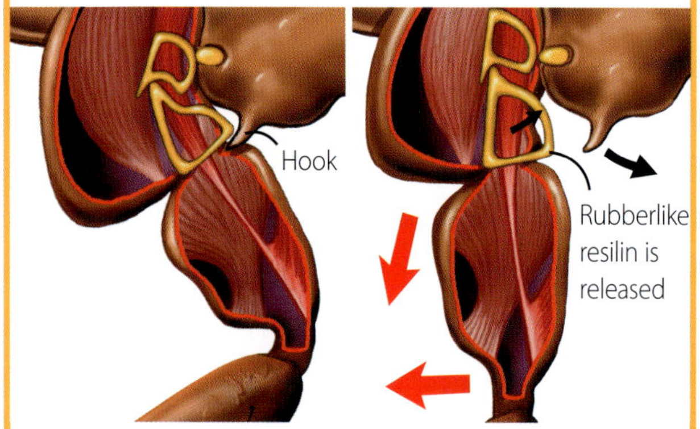


Powerful muscles pull the leg up against a hook on the flea's body, distorting a pad of rubberlike cuticle called resilin. A sideways movement of the top of the leg pulls the hook off the catch, and as the resilin pad springs back into shape (like twanging a stretched elastic band), all the stored energy from the pad is transferred to the flea's toes, catapulting it up to 15 inches (40 cm) into the air.

## Digestion

Ground-up blood from the crop is squirted into the midgut and mixed with enzymes. It then moves back up to the midgut wall, where it is absorbed into the bloodstream.

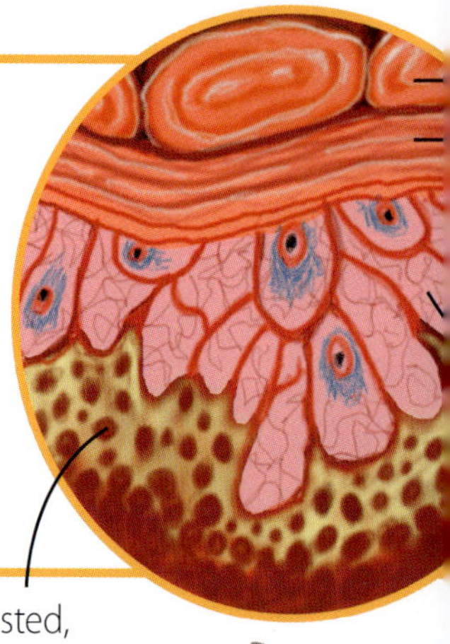

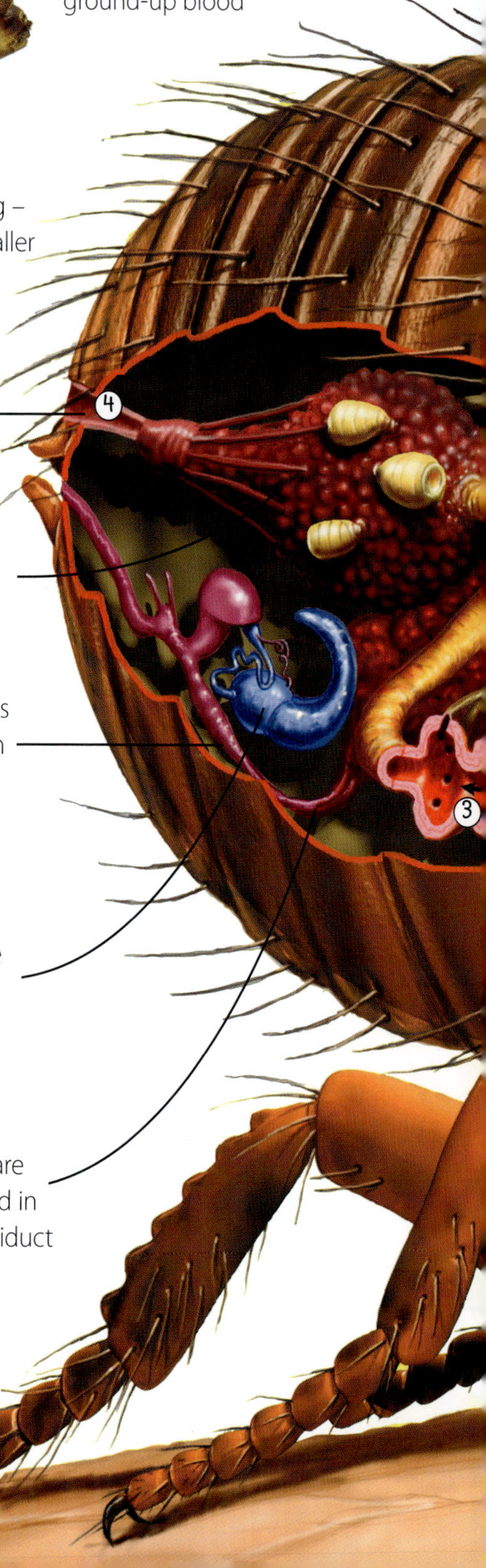

Muscles around the midgut move food back and forth as it is digested

Some cells in the midgut secrete digestive enzymes; others absorb digested food

## Crop

Blood is pumped from the throat into the muscular crop. The crop is lined with sharp, backward-facing spines that grind up the blood cells. Valves stop the blood from being forced out of the crop until it is ready and needed. Once ground up, the contents of the crop are squeezed into the midgut for digestion.

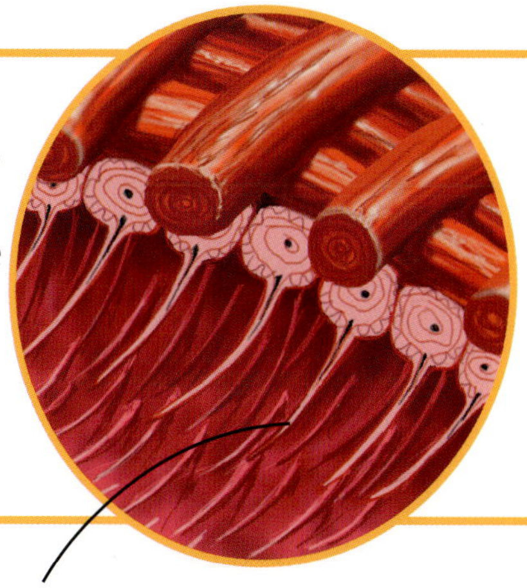


## Feeding on blood

Sharp mandibles bore into the host, then saliva is forced into the wound to prevent the blood from clotting and blocking up the hole. Blood is sucked into the esophagus, through a valve (1), and into the crop. It then passes through another valve (2) into the midgut. A valve (3) releases excess water and waste into the hindgut and rectum where water and salts are taken in. Waste stored in the rectum passes out through the anus (4).

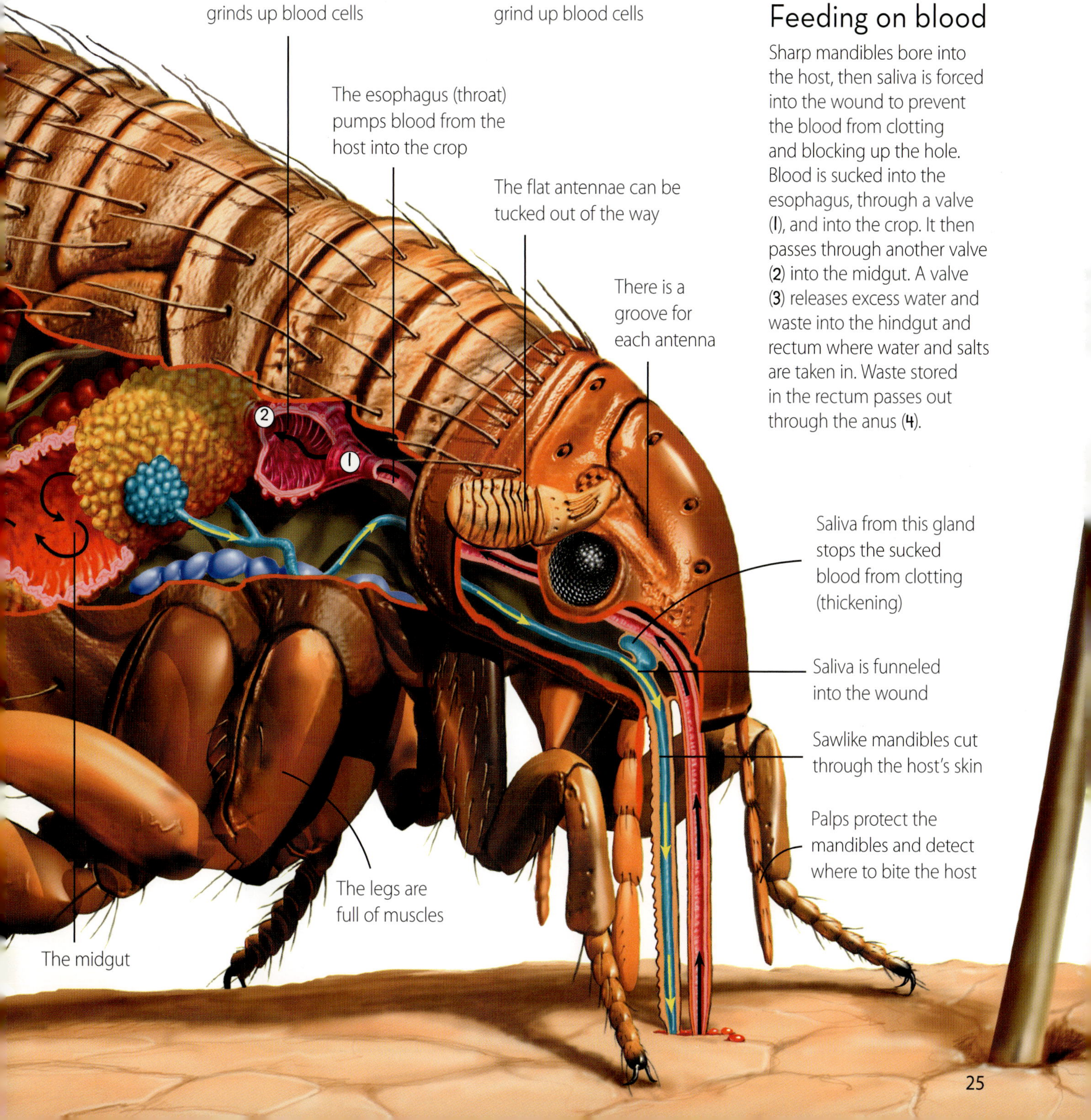

# Mating

An insect's main purpose in life is to reproduce. Some insects do not even feed, they just mate, lay eggs, and die. Like most other female animals, a female insect produces eggs from a pair of ovaries. The eggs travel down to her uterus where they are fertilized by sperm produced by the male. The sperm are made in a pair of organs, called the testes, inside the male.

Some male insects leave packets of sperm on the ground for the female to pick up. However, to ensure the sperm is safe, many transfer their sperm to the female directly. The male insect climbs onto the back of the female (*right*). It then inserts its sex organ into her, to pump sperm into her uterus. The sperm may be used to fertilize eggs right away, or stored in a sac inside the female's body until they are needed.

## Fighting for territory

Rhinoceros beetles get their name because the males are armed with "horns." They fight each other over the possession of a place where females they can mate with are likely to be. They try to turn each other over. The winner claims the territory and the loser leaves.

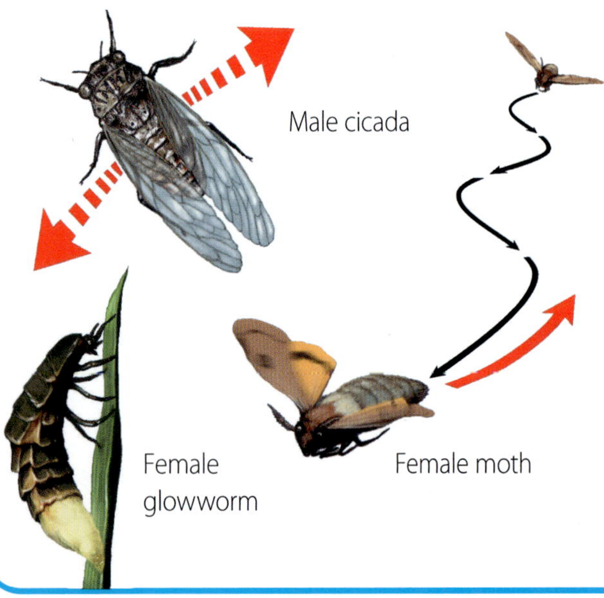


## Ways of finding a mate

Male cicadas use sound to attract a mate. They "sing," which brings the males together and attracts females to them. Other insects find a mate by sight. For example, female glowworms emit light at dusk to attract a mate. And many use smell. The female moth releases tiny amounts of chemicals called pheromones, which can be detected by a male many miles away. He follows the scent to find her.

## Sperm

Each sperm consists of a head and a smaller middle section that drives a vibrating tail, which pushes the sperm along. The head contains chromosomes. These contribute half the instructions to make a new beetle once they have joined with another half, found in a female's egg.

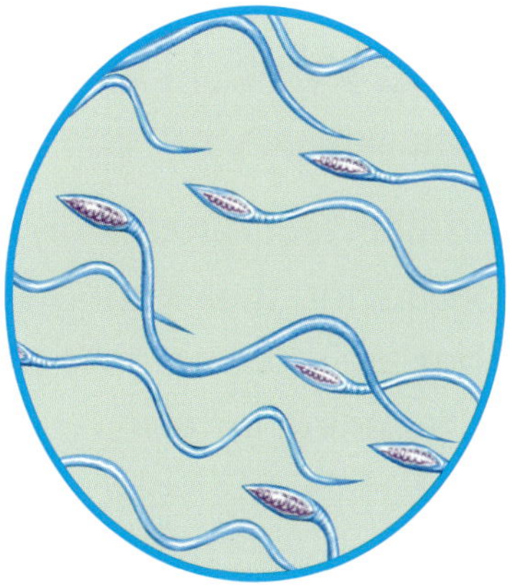

## Male and female organs

In the male beetle, sperm made in the testes (**1**) travel down tubes, and are stored in sacs (**2**). During mating, sperm are forced along a tube (**3**) into the male's sex organ (**4**), then into the female's uterus (**5**) and sperm sac (**6**). The sperm are stored here until they are needed. Eggs from the female's ovaries (**7**) travel down to be fertilized by the sperm before being laid.

# New Life

Adult insects are mainly concerned with producing their young and making sure they are safe and have plenty of food to eat. After being fertilized by a male, the female butterfly finds a place to lay her eggs – a suitable plant that will provide her offspring with food and as much protection from predators as possible.

The female then lays an egg or several eggs. Each egg is filled with a rich yolk for the developing embryo to feed on. It is tough and waterproof to seal in moisture while the egg is exposed to the air. After being laid, it may take between several days and several weeks for the embryo in the egg to develop and hatch, depending on the surrounding temperature.

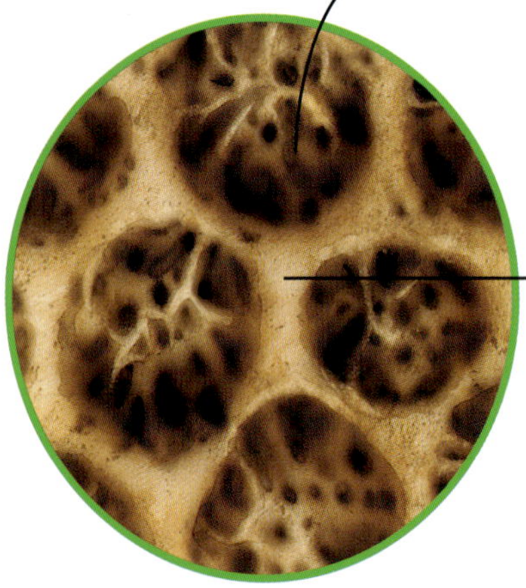


## Eggshell structure

Through a microscope, we can see complicated patterns of pores on the surface of the eggshell. These lead into cavities, which let the egg breathe without losing precious moisture. Many insect eggs allow the developing embryo to breathe in both wet and dry conditions, in case the egg is covered by a raindrop.

## Laying eggs

Each egg consists of a cell that will join with the sperm and grow, and a ball of cells that surround the yolk. The yolk is the developing insect's source of food. Cells in the ovary produce the surrounding eggshell. Before the egg is laid, sperm that has been stored in a pouch enters the egg through a special pore in the eggshell. The female also produces a gluey substance to stick the egg to the plant's surface.

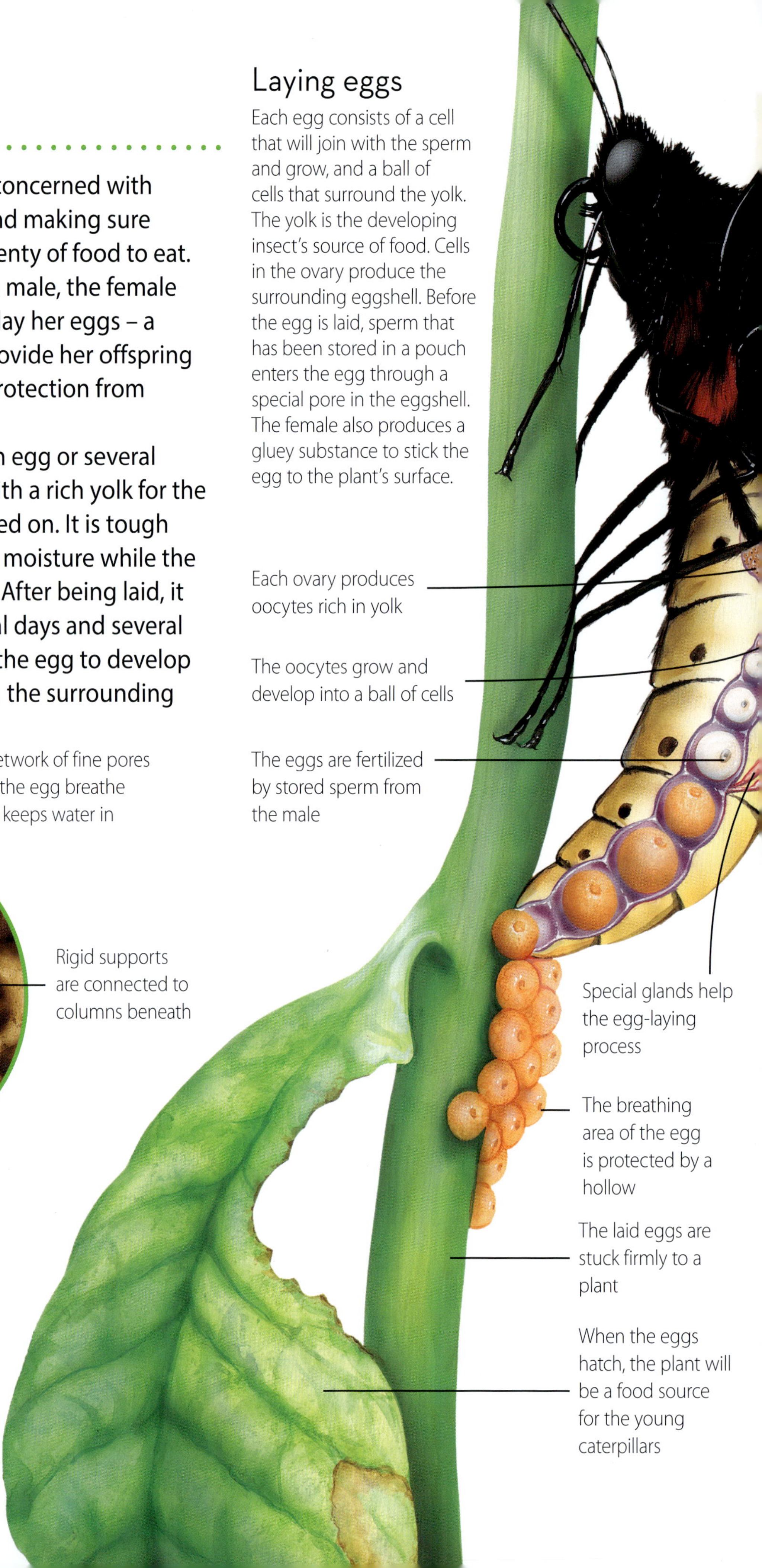

## All sorts of eggs

Lacewing eggs (**1**) are suspended on the ends of fine threads away from predators. Butterflies glue their tiny, flask-shaped eggs (**2**) to plants. Cockroaches lay eight eggs in tough packets called oothecae (**3**). Stick insects' eggs (**4**) have a lid that pops open to release the young, and water scorpions' eggs (**5**) have breathing horns that poke above the surface of the water. For safety, some sawflies lay their eggs (**6**) inside leaves close to the veins.

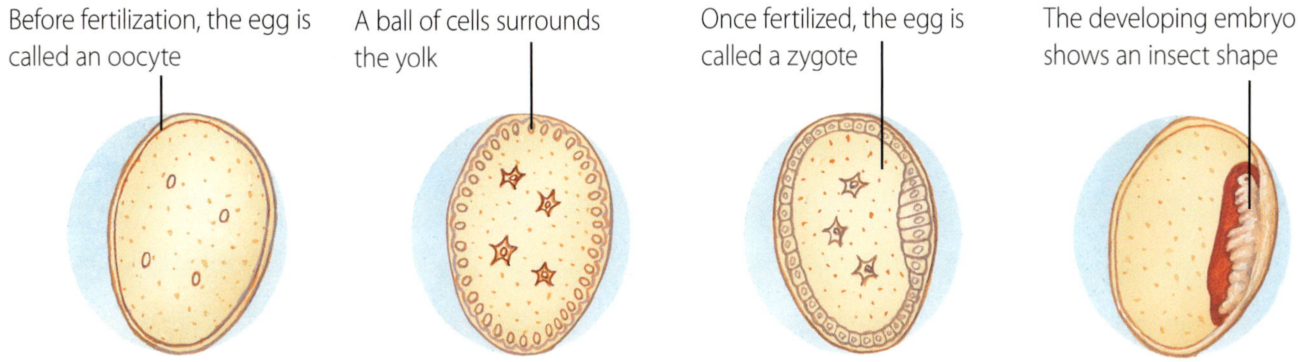


## Embryo development

Some insects have a three-stage life cycle and some go through five stages, but all insects begin life as an egg. Before fertilization, the egg cell divides to form a sphere of cells called an oocyte, with some scattered cells drifting in the yolk. The cells continue to divide. The eggshell is produced by the outer cells. One cell is fertilized by the sperm from the male and the egg is laid. The fertilized cell, called a zygote, divides and forms the embryo, which will develop into the young insect. At this stage, the beginnings of the mouthparts, antennae, and legs can just be seen. Once developed, the egg hatches and either a larva (in a five-stage life cycle) or a nymph (*see page 30*) will crawl out.

# Changing Shape

Many insects hatch from eggs as nymphs, which molt (shed their outer skin) and gradually grow to their adult size. But others, such as butterflies, undergo a total metamorphosis (change) and hatch once from their egg, and a second time from their pupa.

A butterfly's first stage of life is in caterpillar form. Its soft cuticle (outer skin) allows its body to expand as it eats and grows. When the cuticle becomes too tight, it is cast off and a new one forms as the caterpillar continues to get larger. After a few weeks, the caterpillar changes into a chrysalis, or pupa. This is known as the pupal stage. About a month later, the adult butterfly hatches, ready to find a mate and produce more butterflies.

## 8) New butterfly

Immediately after breaking out, the new butterfly has to stretch and expand its wings by pumping blood into the wing veins. The expanded wings then dry out and the butterfly uses them to soar into the air.

## 7) Emergence

About a month after the chrysalis was formed, and the process of change is complete, the adult butterfly emerges from its chrysalis. Puffing itself up with air causes the case to split open, allowing the butterfly to crawl free.

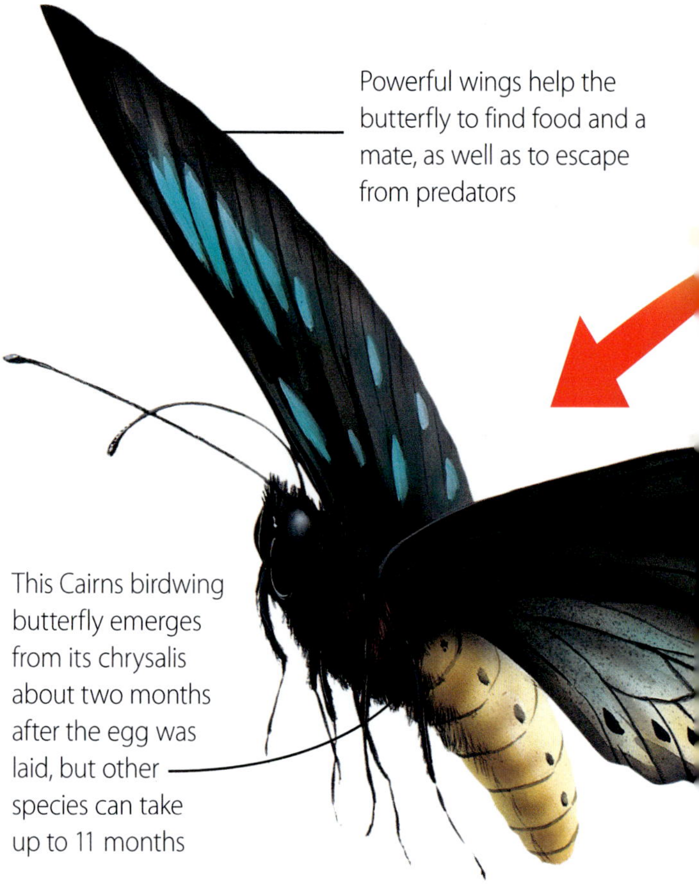


## 1) Eggs

The female butterfly lays clusters of eggs on a plant, which will provide food for the caterpillars after they hatch. The eggshells stick to the leaf and keep the developing caterpillars from drying out.

## 2) Hatching

All the eggs hatch at the same time. The young caterpillar bites a hole in the top of the eggshell, then it crawls out and eats the shell before starting to eat the plant.

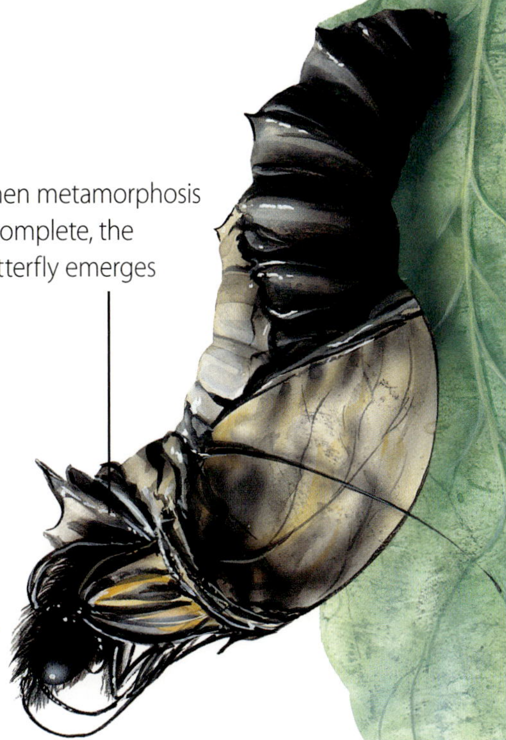


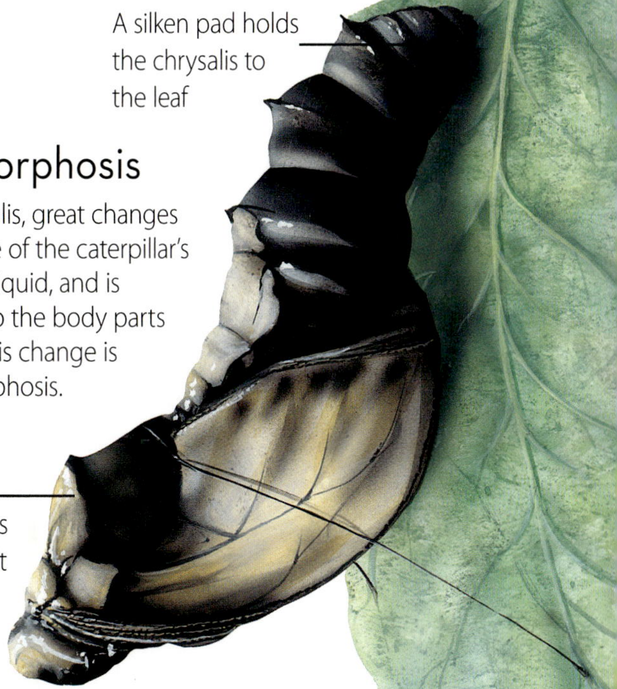


## 6) Metamorphosis

Inside the chrysalis, great changes take place. Some of the caterpillar's body becomes liquid, and is reassembled into the body parts of a butterfly. This change is called metamorphosis.

## 5) Chrysalis

The caterpillar climbs to a safe place, where it spins a silk pad to grip the underside of a leaf, and attaches itself to it with fine hooks. It may also spin a silk loop or hammock to hold itself steady. The caterpillar then sheds its outer skin for a final time, revealing the harder layer of skin, called a chrysalis or pupa, which has developed inside.

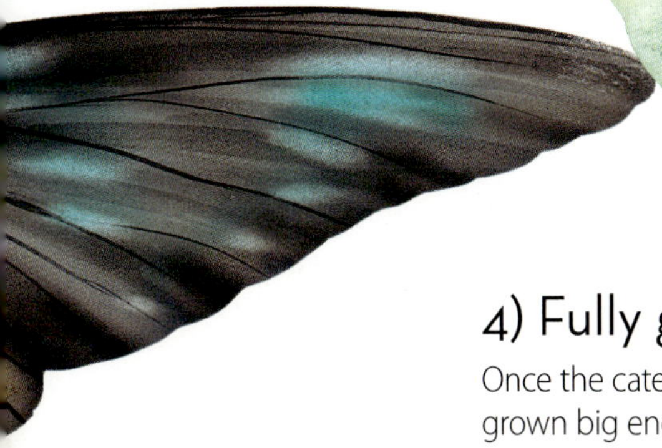

## 4) Fully grown

Once the caterpillar has grown big enough, its body starts to change inside. It then seeks out somewhere safe to pupate (change into a chrysalis) for the final transformation to take place.

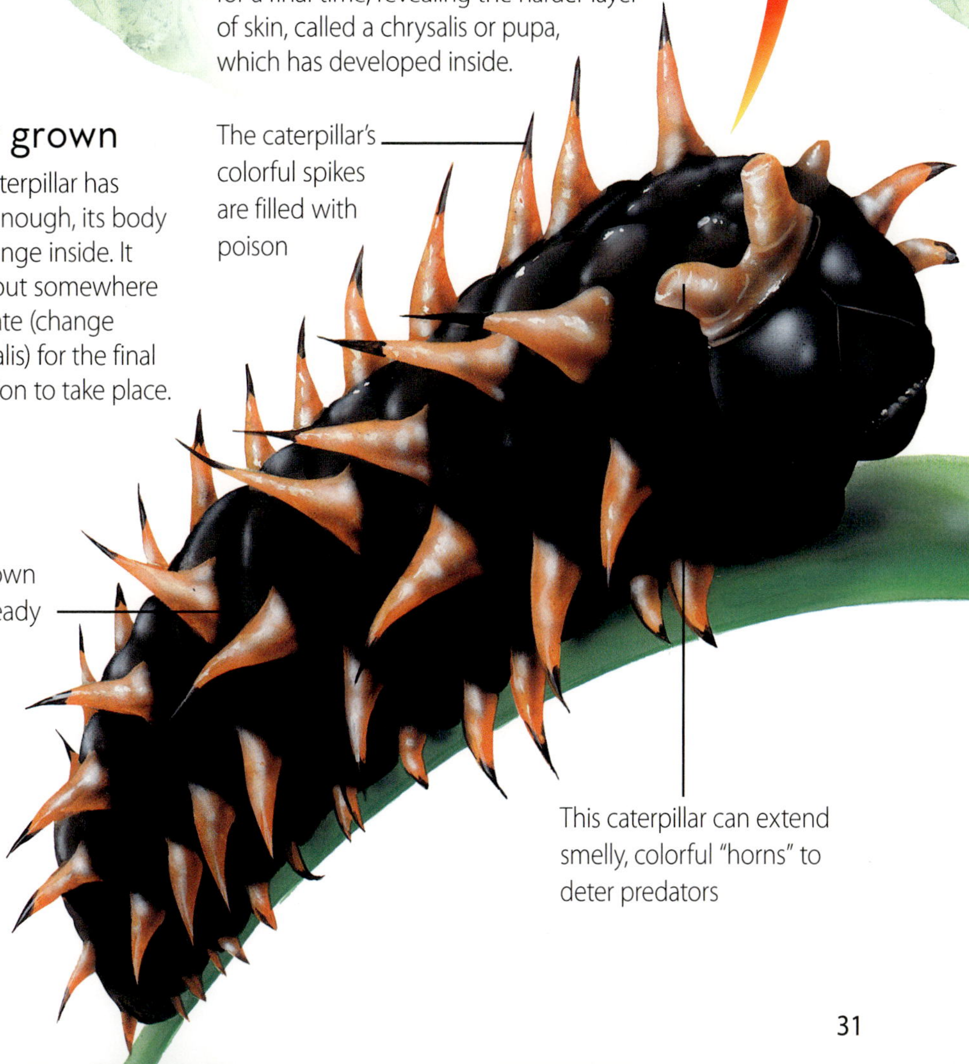


## 3) Shedding skin

As it grows, the caterpillar's skin becomes too tight. It has to shed it for a larger one. It does this by sucking in air to expand itself and split its old skin, exposing the new skin that has grown underneath.

# Ant Nest

Ants live together in complex societies. There are over 5,000 different kinds of ant community. Each nest is headed by a queen that is cared for by female workers. Some ants have different types of workers, called castes, which do different tasks. Ants build their nests in all kinds of places. Here, the nest is both above and below the ground. Workers burrow in the soil and pile up the material they dig out on the surface above. The mound itself is then dug with tunnels and chambers too, which connect with the ones belowground. In this maze, the queen ant lives, the eggs and larvae are cared for, and food is stored. At certain times, winged queens and males are produced. These leave the nest in mass swarms several times every summer to mate.

## Egg-laying queen

The queen is much larger than her workers. She is the only ant in the nest that lays eggs. As the eggs are laid, they are looked after by attendant workers. On hatching, the young larvae are moved to other chambers where they become pupae (chrysalises). Ants will emerge from the pupae.

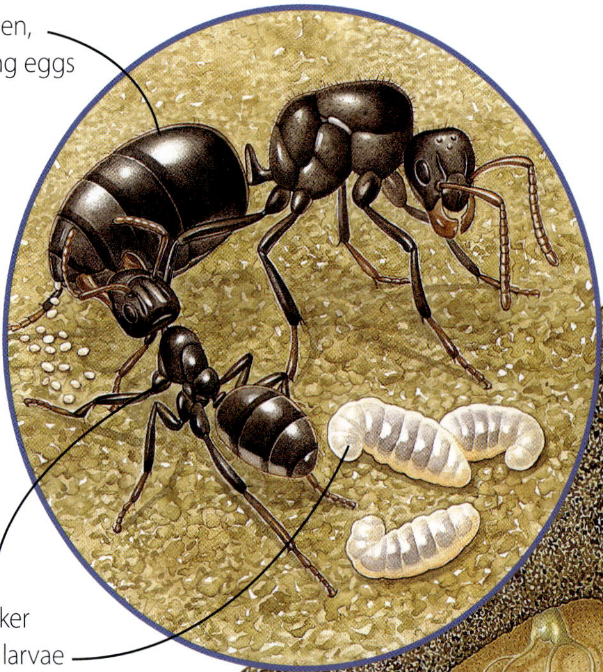

Queen, laying eggs

Worker and larvae

A worker ant collecting honeydew from an aphid

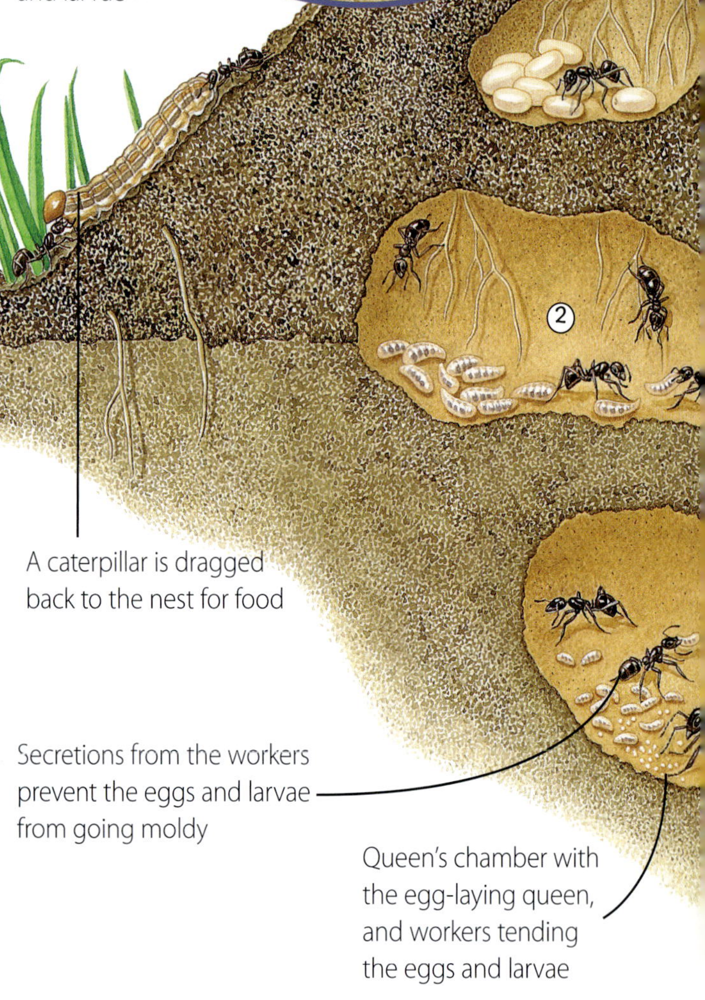


A caterpillar is dragged back to the nest for food

Secretions from the workers prevent the eggs and larvae from going moldy

Queen's chamber with the egg-laying queen, and workers tending the eggs and larvae

## Herding aphids

To feed, tiny insects called aphids suck plant sap. This sap contains a lot of water and sugar, far more than the aphids need, so they pass out the excess. Ants have a sweet tooth and collect this sugary liquid, which is called honeydew. To make the aphids produce more, the ants direct aphids to the juiciest parts of plants, and stroke their backs. The ants also look after the aphids, guarding them from predators.

## Ant variety

Ants eat plants, honeydew, nectar, and fungi, as well as other insects. Some species of ants collect honeydew, which they feed to special workers whose abdomens swell like grapes, making them into living honeypots! Leafcutter ants eat the fungus that grows on the plant pieces they collect. Harvester ants collect seeds, dry them in the sun, then store them to eat later.

Honeypot ants

Leafcutter ants

Harvester ants

## Ants' home life

An ant mound absorbs the sun's heat, keeping the nest warm. In the royal chamber (**1**), the queen lays eggs, which are taken to other chambers (**2**) to be cared for. The larvae are moved to nursery chambers (**3**) where they will change into pupae. Other chambers are food stores. Tunnels connect the chambers and let workers get to the outside to forage.

# Bee Nest

Honeybee nests are busy places. In each nest, a bustling community of up to 60,000 insects live together. Nearly all the bees are females, called workers, which hatch from fertilized eggs laid by the queen that is in charge of the colony. Only males (known as drones) hatch from unfertilized eggs. They appear in the summer and autumn. They do not work, as their only job is to mate with new queens.

All the worker bees live together, building and looking after their home, collecting food and water, feeding the young, and caring for the queen. They secrete wax to make their nest. Sheets of strong, hexagonal cells hang down and hold the eggs, larvae, nectar (which becomes honey), and pollen. Being able to store food allows honeybees to live through times when food is scarce, such as in winter.

## Building cells

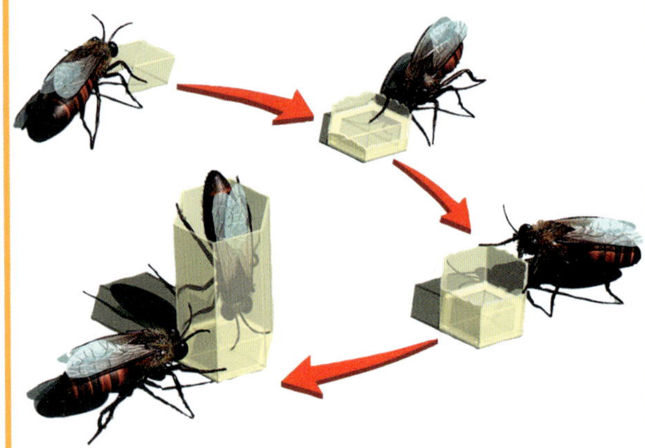

A worker bee produces scales of wax from glands under its abdomen. These are spread onto a surface using its jaws. More wax is added and shaped into a hexagonal cell. Cells are produced together, forming a sheet of honeycomb with cells on both sides, each angled slightly upwards. Combs of these cells hang side by side, just close enough to allow two bees to pass each other.

## Queen

A queen can lay over 2,000 eggs a day. At certain times, some of these are laid in special large cells. Larvae from these eggs get extra food and grow into young queens. When they are about to hatch, the old queen leaves the nest with the older workers. This "swarm" sets up home elsewhere and the new queen takes over the old nest.

## Waggle dance

A bee can tell other bees where it has found a lot of food by dancing. The angle it dances at tells the other bees which direction to go in to find it. The faster the bee waggles, the more food there is. The number of turns she makes in a given time indicates the distance they must go.

# Rainforest Life

Tropical heat and moisture are ideal for the growth of rainforests. Here, insects are the most numerous and varied form of animal life. Nearly 200 species of butterflies can be found in 2.5 acres (1 ha) of Southeast Asian rainforest. However, we do not know how many rainforest insects there are in total – there may still be millions to discover.

Insects can be difficult to see as many fly high in the treetops, and many are so well camouflaged that they look just like a flower, thorn, or leaf. Others live hidden inside rotting wood, living plants, or leaves. Insects are a very important part of forest life – they pollinate plants and help to recycle waste matter into reusable nutrients.

## Mantis

This is not a pretty flower, but a dangerous predator! Disguised to match the flower upon which it sits, this mantis waits patiently for an insect to visit the flower – then it will pounce.

## Grasshoppers

Powerful back legs allow grasshoppers to jump out of the way of danger. These green nymphs are well camouflaged and difficult to see in the forest.

## Leafcutter ants

Strong leafcutter ants cut pieces of leaves and carry them to their nest. They eat the fungus that begins to grow on the leaf pieces.

## Pond in a tree

The bases of the leaves of bromeliads, which include the pineapple, wrap around the stem and trap water. These form ponds in which many creatures live.

## Pitcher plant ants

The hollow, coiled base of a pitcher plant stem makes a safe place for these ants to live and rear their young. In return for their home, the ants guard the pitcher plant against attack by insects and other animals.

## Weavers

Ants nest everywhere in the rainforest. Even living leaves can be made into a home. Weaver ant larvae secrete sticky silk. These larvae are used like tubes of glue by the ants to bind the leaves together.

## Termites

Dead leaves and wood collect on the dark forest floor. They are eaten by all kinds of creatures. Termites gather dead leaves and take them back to their nest.

## Great Mormon butterfly

Many butterflies have wings that camouflage them when at rest. If disturbed, a move of the wings exposes colorful markings that can frighten a predator.

# Insects in Water

Many types of insects live in fresh water at some time in their lives. Several, including flies such as the dragonfly as well as true flies, only spend the earliest part of their lives there – as nymphs (young that resemble the adult insect) or larvae (a wormlike form that does not resemble the adult until later on).

Other freshwater insects, like beetles and bugs, live in water both during their early and adult stages. The adults also live on land, traveling through the air to new habitats. Because large amounts of dissolved oxygen can be found in water, many insects are able to breathe in it. Most nymphs use gills to breathe, but other insects breathe at the water's surface. A few take a pocket of air down with them when they dive, returning to the surface to get more when the oxygen runs out. Insects use their legs and even their wings to swim around.

## A mayfly's life

Mayfly nymphs feed on dead vegetation and live in tubes in mud or crawl among aquatic plants. As adults, they have just a day to live. During that time, they do not eat but only mate and lay eggs.

A mayfly

Whirligig beetles spin around on the surface looking for food

Mosquito larvae and pupae breathe through the surface film of the water

Air is trapped under the great diving beetle's wing covers

It has broad, oar-like back legs for swimming

Its legs push against the water, forcing the beetle forward

The diving beetle's strong front legs can grasp prey

## Great diving beetle

During adulthood and as larvae, these beetles are fast, aggressive predators. Adults are sleek and smooth, and have broad, oar-like back legs, fringed with bristles for rapid swimming. Their front legs are adapted to grasping their prey. When they are undewater, they breathe using air trapped in hairs beneath their wing covers.

## Life cycle of a dragonfly

The dragonfly lays its eggs underwater, in or on water plants. The eggs hatch as predatory nymphs (**1**). As each nymph grows, it molts and gradually changes. Eventually it crawls out of the water (**2**) and emerges as an adult dragonfly with tiny wings (**3**), which it inflates and dries before flying off in search of food or a mate (**4**).

## Life on the surface

The surface of the water, known as the surface film, is home to several insect hunters and scavengers. Tiny wingless springtails called podura (**5**) scavenge for food. Aptly named pond skaters (**6**) are fast hunters, but they will also take trapped and drowned prey. The water boatman (**7**) hangs from the surface of the water waiting for prey. Using its powerful legs, it chases its victim, killing it with its stabbing mouthparts.

## A "masked" hunter

A hungry dragonfly nymph catches its prey using a special mouthpart, known as a "mask." The mask stays folded under the head until the nymph shoots it forward and catches the prey using the strong jaws at its tip.

# Woodland Life

Trees make perfect homes for many insects, providing plenty of food and places to shelter. One tree in particular, the oak, supports a huge variety of insect life, including over 210 species of moths and butterflies. Insects make use of all of the tree – from the leaves, shoots, and flowers in the canopy to the roots underground. They chew the leaves from the outside and inside, burrow under the bark and into the wood, and live inside the tree's fruits, acorns. As well as eating the tree, they also use it as a refuge, hiding in crevices in the bark.

Some insects are parasites, living on the insects that feed on the tree. Others are predators, searching and hunting for prey. Throughout the year, different insects can be found on different parts of every tree in a woodland or forest.

## Marble gall

Gall wasps have two types of larvae. Those of one species produce marble galls on one type of oak and bud galls on another.

## Purple hairstreak

This butterfly only lives on oak. Its caterpillars feed at night on young leaves. When fully grown they pupate in the soil. If taken into an ant nest they are better protected from predators.

## Oak bark beetle

Just below the bark a female beetle makes a tunnel where she lays her eggs. The grubs that hatch make long vertical tunnels as they feed.

## Acorn weevil

Like all nut weevils, the acorn weevil has a long, thin snout. At its tip are mandibles, which it uses to pierce a hole and bore into the acorn. Here it lays an egg, and the grub (larva) feeds in its ready-made pantry. When the acorn falls, the grub comes out and develops into a pupa in the soil.

## Lacewing

Delicate lacewings are active in the evening. Both adults and larvae hunt aphids. The larvae camouflage themselves by sticking pieces of debris to their back, including the dried husks of their prey.

## Oak sawfly

Sawflies are related to bees and wasps. Their larvae are sluglike caterpillars. Oak sawfly caterpillars produce blistering marks as they feed on the underside of the leaf.

## Thorn moth

Adult moths are well camouflaged – their brown, jagged wings look like dead leaves. If a thorn moth caterpillar is disturbed or at rest, it makes itself look (very convincingly) like a twig.

## Lobster moth

When resting, the lobster moth caterpillar has a strange appearance, hence its name. Although it eats oak leaves, it will also eat the leaves of other trees.

## Seven-spotted ladybug

Most ladybugs are predators. As larvae and adults they eat huge numbers of sap-sucking aphids. Their bright colors warn predators that they taste nasty and should not be eaten.

## Dark crimson underwing moth

When at rest, with its wings folded, this moth is perfectly camouflaged on the oak tree's bark. Its caterpillars eat oak buds and pupate amongst the lichen on the tree trunk.

## Types of gall

Some insects and larvae inject small amounts of chemicals into trees. The trees then produce balls of thickened tissue called galls that limit the damage to the tree, and provide food and shelter for the larvae. Different species of gall wasps produce different types of galls, such as curved leaf galls (1), cotton-wool galls (**2**), spangle galls (**3**), and oak apples (**4**).

# Desert Insects

Deserts are mainly hot and dry, having little rainfall, so the environment is a difficult one for animals to survive in. Those that do are specially adapted to the harsh conditions. Many hide away during the extreme heat of the day, either under rocks, buried in the sand, or deep in burrows.

Only at night and early morning, when it is cool, do they emerge to feed. Those insects that do come out during the day move from place to place quickly, keeping in the shade. Their feet are often specially adapted so that they are able to touch the hot sand when necessary, and they have a thick cuticle to reduce the loss of moisture. Some gather moisture to drink in the early morning mist, while others rely on the moisture in their food to sustain them. Even if they do lose water they can withstand a great deal of dehydration (water loss).

## Dune cricket

The dune cricket (**3**) uses its flower-shaped feet to dig in the sand to escape predators and the heat of the sun. When the temperature falls, the cricket emerges to feed on the sparse vegetation.

## Head-stander

Water droplets from early morning mist condense on this darkling beetle (**5**). It stands on tiptoe so the droplets run together and down to its mouth.

## Tiger beetle

Like a tiger in the jungle, a tiger beetle (**4**) hunts its prey. These agile and fast predators have powerful jaws to kill even quite large insects.

## Hunting wasp

A hunting wasp lives a solitary life. A female (**1**) digs a burrow and then hunts for insects. Using her sting, she paralyzes her prey and takes it back to the burrow. Here she lays an egg on it. The larva that hatches feeds on the living victim.

## Harvester ants

Harvester ants (**2**) nest underground, away from the sun's intense heat. Foragers gather seeds for food, which they first dry in the sun before storing them in special chambers inside their nest. They eat the seeds as needed. They also eat insects such as caterpillars.

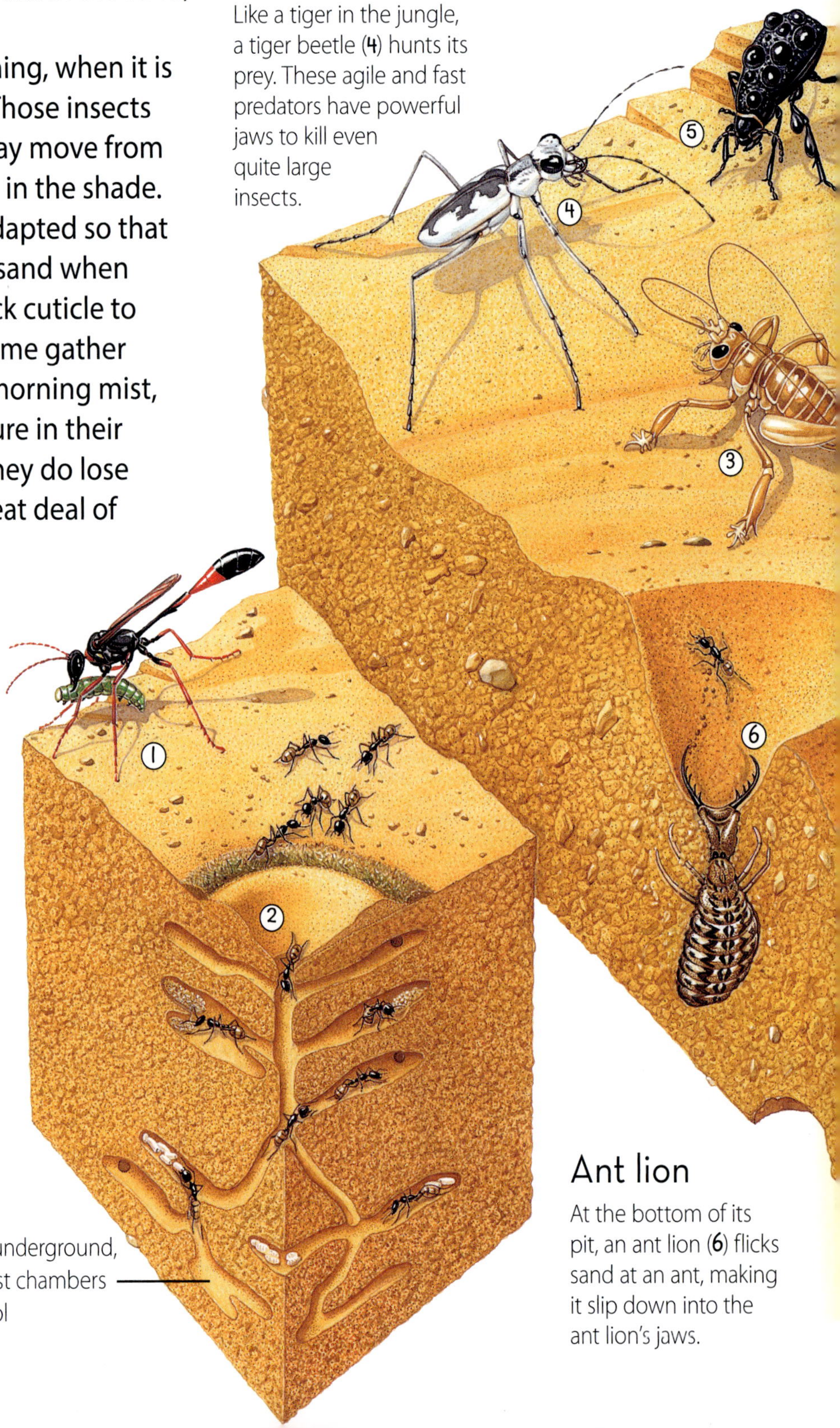


## Ant lion

At the bottom of its pit, an ant lion (**6**) flicks sand at an ant, making it slip down into the ant lion's jaws.

## Eburnea beetle

Most darkling beetles are black, so this one is unusual in being white (**7**). Darkling beetles form a large part of the desert fauna. Their hard, thick armor protects them from desiccation (drying up).

## Long-legged beetle

Extra long legs allow this darkling beetle (**8**) to move fast and keep its body well clear of the hot desert sand. Moisture gathers on its back in the early morning.

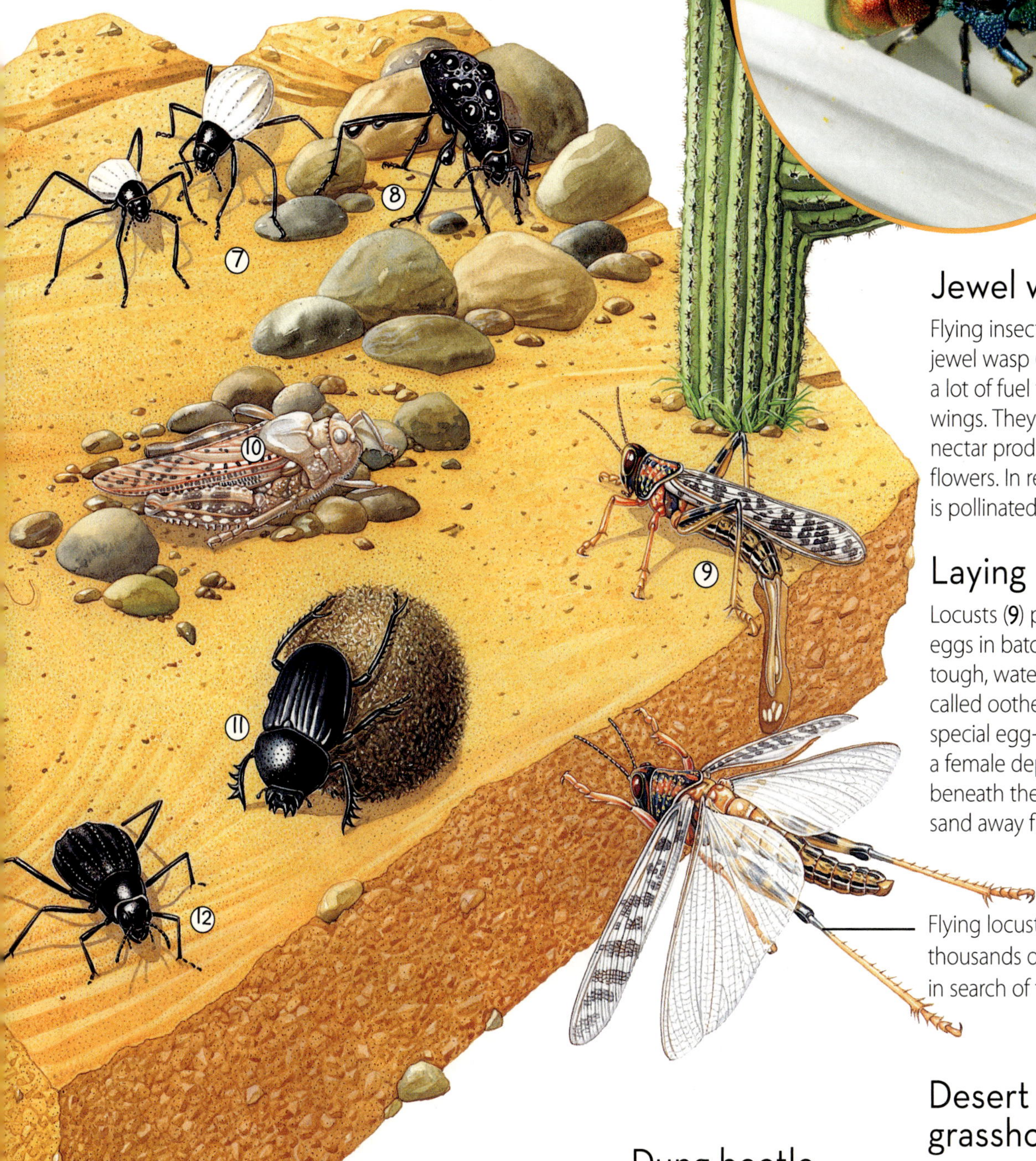


Flying locusts can travel thousands of miles (km) in search of food

## Jewel wasp

Flying insects, such as the jewel wasp (*above*), need a lot of fuel to work their wings. They get this from nectar produced by desert flowers. In return, the plant is pollinated.

## Laying eggs

Locusts (**9**) produce their eggs in batches inside tough, waterproof packages called oothecae. Using a special egg-laying tube, a female deposits these beneath the surface of the sand away from predators.

## Darkling beetle

Most species of darkling beetles are a dull black (**12**), but their body shape can differ greatly. The majority are nocturnal scavengers that feed largely on plant remains.

## Dung beetle

Dung beetles (**11**) gather dung into balls, roll it to safety, and bury it. Underground, they lay their eggs on the dung so the larvae that hatch have a plentiful food source.

## Desert grasshopper

Is it a stone? No, it's a desert grasshopper (**10**). These grasshoppers live wherever there is sufficient plant life. To avoid being eaten, they are well camouflaged to resemble the stones of the surrounding desert.

# Microscopic Life

Hidden away in their secret worlds are thousands of microscopic insects. Insects are the most successful group of living animals on Earth partly because many of them make use of the tiniest of spaces – including the gaps between grains of cereal, the crevices in tree bark, and in the fur of mammals.

Within most groups of insects there are species that are microscopic. Despite their tiny size, they have the same body design as their larger relatives. Due to their small body size, breathing is easy as oxygen and carbon dioxide have only a very short distance to travel between the surrounding atmosphere and the inside of the insect's body. They also require very little food and moisture to survive. But as they cannot carry or store much energy, quick or energy-intense movement, like flying, is usually done only in short bursts.

## Head louse

Head lice are a type of sucking lice that live in human hair. More than a thousand can live on one head, but the normal number is about a dozen. For camouflage they match the color of the hair in which they live. Anyone can be a host to lice, catching them from other people and clothing. When feeding, the louse grabs a hair and stands on its head, gripping the scalp with a ring of hooks, before inserting a long mouthpart into the skin to suck blood. They feed twice a day, causing irritation and sometimes disease.

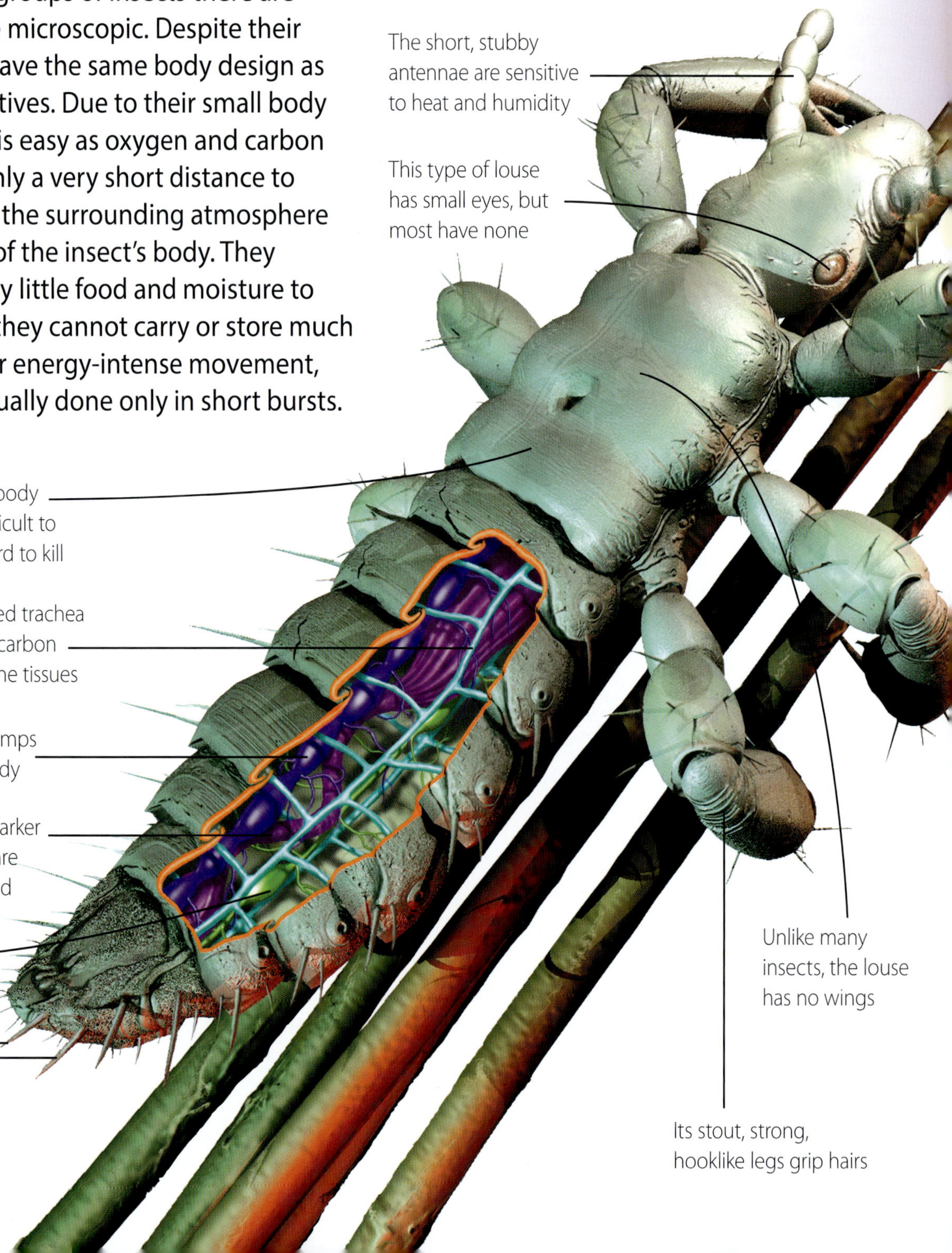

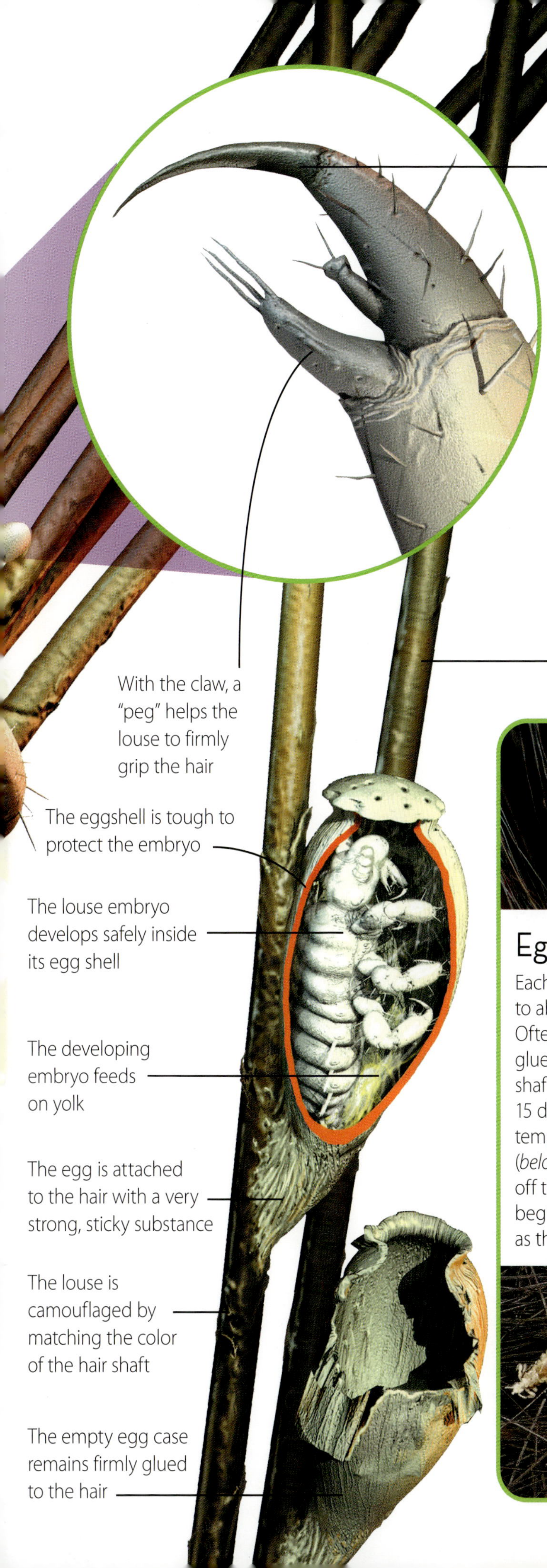


## Climbing feet

A head louse's feet are covered with spines and have curved, hinged claws that grip onto hair with the help of a "peg." The claws give the louse a very strong hold and make climbing hair easy. They also make it difficult for the host to remove the louse.

## Eggs

Each day, head lice lay up to about eight eggs (*above*). Often called nits, each is glued very firmly to a hair shaft. The eggs hatch in 6 to 15 days, depending on the temperature. The young lice (*below*) hatch by pushing off the egg's cap, and they begin to suck blood as soon as they reach the host's skin.

## Fairyfly

Less than a quarter of a millimeter long, fairyflies are the smallest of all insects. They are wasps that lay their eggs in other insects. Aquatic species can use their wings for swimming.

## Springtail

Springtails can spring several inches (cm). Normally the springing organ is tucked under the abdomen, secured by a special hook. When released, it catapults the insect into the air.

## Silverfish

Silverfish are covered in fine, gleaming scales. They hide away, usually appearing indoors at night to eat paper, leather, and food scraps.

# Index


A
abdomen 6–9, 15
antennae 6, 8, 12–13, 17, 23, 25, 27, 44
ant lions 42
ant nests 32–33, 36, 37, 42
ants 17, 32–33, 36, 37, 42
anus 22, 23, 24
aphids 32
armor plating 6, 8–9

B
bee nests 34–35
bees 18, 22
beetles 8–12, 14, 17, 20, 18–19, 26–27, 38, 40, 42, 43
blood 6, 22–25, 30, 44
bombardier beetles 18–19
brain 6, 7, 8, 10, 11, 13
breathing 6, 7
bugs 37, 38
bush crickets 22
butterflies 14, 20, 22, 29, 30, 36, 37, 40

C
ceca 23
camouflage 16, 18, 20, 36
caterpillars 18, 21, 28, 30, 31, 32, 42
chemicals 18, 19, 26, 34
chitin 6, 8
chrysalis (pupa) 30–33, 35, 38
cicadas 26
claws 9, 16, 24, 27, 45
cockchafer beetles 12
cockroaches 22–23, 29
colon 22
color 11, 18, 20–21
crickets 22, 42
crop 6, 23, 25
cuticle 6–9, 13, 14, 18, 20, 30, 42

D
damselflies 11
darkling beetles 42, 43
desert insects 42–43
digestion 6, 7, 22–23, 24
dragonflies 12, 14, 39
dune crickets 42
dung beetles 43

E
eardrums 7
earwigs 12
eggs 12, 24, 26–30, 32–35, 42, 43, 45
epidermis 9
esophagus 22, 25
excretion 7, 19
exoskeleton 6, 8, 9, 24
eyes 6, 8, 10–11, 16, 17, 18, 44

F
fairyflies 45
feelers *see antennae*
feet 9, 13, 42
fertilization 27, 28, 29, 34
fleas 24–25
flies 10, 11, 14
flowers 11, 17
flying 14–15
food 6, 7, 22–23, 24, 32–35

G
galls 40, 41
gizzard 6, 22, 23
glowworms 26
grasshoppers 7, 36, 43
great diving beetles 38
gut 22, 23, 24, 25

H
hatching 30
head 6, 8, 16, 17
head lice 44–45
heart 6, 44
hinges 9
honey 33, 34, 35
honeybees 34–35
houseflies 22
hunting 16–17

I
ileum 22
intestines 7, 19, 44

J
jaws (mandibles) 6, 8, 16, 17, 18, 25, 39, 42
jewel wasps 43
joints 9, 14

L
lacewings 29, 40
ladybugs 41
larvae 32, 33, 34, 37, 38–39, 40, 41, 43
leaf insects 37
legs 6–9, 15–18, 21, 24, 44
locusts 6–7, 43

M
mantises 16–17, 36
mating 26–27, 32
maxilla 8
mayflies 38
microscopic life 44–45
molting 30, 31
mosquitoes 22, 38
moths 12, 18, 26, 40, 41
mouth 6, 8, 11, 22
muscles 8, 9, 14, 17, 19, 25

N
nectar 34
nerve cells 7, 10
nymphs 38, 39

O
ocelli 10
ommatidia 10, 11
oocytes 28, 29
optic nerves 11
ovaries 26, 27, 28

P
parasites 24–25
poison 18, 36, 37
pollen 34, 35
pond skaters 39
praying mantises 16–17

R
rainforests 38–39
rectum 7, 19, 22, 24, 25
rhabdom 10

S
saliva 22, 23, 25
sawflies 12, 29, 41
scales 21
segments 8
self-defense 18–19
sense organs 8, 12
sensory cells 13
sensory pegs 13
shield bugs 37
silverfish 45
sperm 24, 26, 27, 28
spines 18, 36
spotted flower beetle 8
springtails 12, 39, 45
stag beetles 17
stick insects 21, 29
sting 18, 42

T
tarsus 9
taste hairs 23
termites 12, 18, 37
testes 26, 27
thorax 8, 14, 15, 17, 22
thornbugs 36
tiger beetles 17, 42
trachea 6, 44
treehoppers 36

U
uterus 26, 27

V
vagina 24

W
waggle dance 35
wasps 12, 14–15, 42, 43, 45
waste 22, 23
water boatmen 39
water insects 38–39
water scorpions 29
weevils 12, 40
whirligig beetles 10, 11, 38
wings 7, 8, 9, 14–15, 16, 20, 21, 30
woodland life 40–41

Z
zygotes 29